THE MYSTERY
OF THE
OLIVE TREE

Published in 2019 by
New Life Publishing, Luton,
Bedfordshire LU4 9HG

On application to him, the author will be willing to give permission for parts of this book to be reproduced in part or in whole to promote the values of the book and for other teachings. On application, the author will also authorise other language translation rights.
email for authorisation to:
pavol.strezo@gmail.com (Pavol Strežo)

British Library Cataloguing in Publication Data
A catalogue record for this book is available
from the British Library

ISBN 978 1 912237 15 9

Unless otherwise stated Bible references are from New International Version © 1973, the International Bible Society, and are used with permission.

Typesetting by New Life Publishing,
Luton, UK   www.goodnewsbooks.co.uk
Printed and bound in Great Britain

The Mystery
of the
Olive Tree

Uniting Jews and Gentiles
for Christ's Return

Johannes Fichtenbauer

I dedicate this book to the memory
of Fr. Peter Hocken, who was my
close friend and spiritual guide.
He taught me to understand
the mystery of Messianic Jews in the
light of the second coming of the Lord.

CONTENTS

Chapter 1
Why Care About Israel? 1
- A Joke with Lots of Meaning 1
- The Jews – the World's Destiny 2
- The Mystery of Israel's Election 4
- A Second Conversion 8
- My Personal Conversion to Israel 11

Chapter 2
All Blessings are mediated through Israel 17
- The Jewish Remnant 19
- The First Council of Jerusalem 21
- Understanding the Mystery of the Olive Tree 24
- Gentiles Depend on Israel – Israel Depends
                         on the Gentiles 26

Chapter 3
A History of Replacement 29
- The Jews Separate Themselves from the Nazarenes .. 30
- The First Division in the Church 33
- The Drama of Replacement Theology 34
      The Letter to Barnabas 36
      Irenaeus of Lyon 36
      Origen 36
      Ambrose 36
      Augustine 37
      John Chrysostom 37

continued......

......*continued*

- From Replacement Theology to Anti-Semitic Politics ... 38
    - Emperor Constantine 38
    - Synod of Elvira/Spain 38
    - Synod of Laodicea 39
    - Council of Chalcedon 39
    - Emperor Theodosius II 39
    - II Council of Nicea 39
    - Martin Luther 41
- The End of Messianic Judaism – the Jewish part
  of the Church 42
- A Limited Ability to Interpret the Hebrew Scriptures ... 44
    - Jerome 44

Chapter 4
The Miracle of Resurrection –
The Messianic Jews of Today 49
- Four Rabbis and One Purpose 49
- The Origin of the Modern Messianic Jewish Movement. 53
    - The 'Christian Hebrew Movement' 54
    - Joseph Rabinowitz 56
- The Horror of the Holocaust Opened a Window
  of Opportunity 57
    - An Independent State of Israel 58
- David against Goliath 58
- Old Testament Prophecies Fulfilled 59

Chapter 5
Messianic Jews in the World Today 63
- Messianic Potential in Ethiopia 65
- Marrano History in South America and the Potential
  for the Movement .. 66

continued......

......*continued*

- The Horror of the Inquisition 67
- What Characterises Messianic Jews Today? 69
    - Christology 69
    - Trinity 70
    - Baptism and Lord's Supper 70
    - Leadership 70
    - The role of Biblical Scriptures 71
    - Real Jews 71
        - Circumcision 72
        - Kashrut 72
        - Family rituals 72
        - Jewish Feasts and Holidays 72
    - Law and Redemption 73
- Not everyone calling himself a Messianic Jew
                                                    is Indeed One 75
- Messianic Jews and Torah 76
    - The Neo-Ebionites 76
    - The Neo-Nazarenes 77
    - Messianic Jewish Orthodoxy 78
    - Evangelical Messianic Judaism 78
    - Jesus-Only Jews 79

Chapter 6
A Catholic Dialogue with the Messianic Jews 81
- A Terrible History of the Catholic Church's Dealing
                                                    with the Jews ... 81
- The Role of Pope John XXIII to Bring a Breakthrough .. 82
- The work of the Post-Nostra-Aetate Popes 85
    Vatican Commission for Religious Relations
                                                    with the Jews 1974 85
    John Paul II 86

continued......

......*continued*

    Notes on the Correct Way to Present Jews and Judaism
        in Catechesis in the Roman Catholic Church.... 87
    Dominus Jesus 87
    Vatican Commission for Religious Relations
                with the Jews 2011 88
- Torah Christology & Israel-Ecclesiology 88
- Encounter in the Vatican 91

Chapter 7
A Challenge for the Gentile Churches 95
- Understanding the Mystery of the Olive Tree 95
- The Messianic Jewish Movement
    an Authentic Phenomenon 96
- Overcoming and Renouncing all Forms of
    Replacement Theology in the Churches 97
- Recognition and Confession of all the Sins
    Against the Jewish People 99
- Representative Confession and Repentance 101
- Overcoming the Sins Against the Jewish
    Part of the Church 103
- A Spiritual Battle 104

- The Church should see the Messianic Jews as an
    Eschatological Sign CCC 674 104
- Relating to the Messianic Jewish Movement in the
    Right Way 107
    Welcome the Messianic Jews 107
    Friendship 107
    Recognition 108
    Loyalty 108
    Acceptance of the Potential 109
    Acknowledgment of the 'Older Brothers' 109

continued......

......*continued*

    Respect for their Autonomy 110
    Freedom and Space 110
    Transmission of 'Spiritual Treasure' 110
    Support 111
    Intercession for the Leadership 111
    Discernment of Spirits 111
    Advocacy within the Gentile World 112
• The Work of the Holy Spirit 112

Chapter 8
The Initiative 'Towards a Second Council of Jerusalem' (TJCII) 115
• The Vision of TJCII – The One New Man 117
• A Moving Tabernacle 117
• The Elders of Jerusalem 118
• The International TJCII Office in Dallas 119
• Intercession 119
• Theology 119
• Diplomatic Work 120
• Promotion 120
    Working on all Continents 120
• The 'Now Generation' 122

Chapter 9
The Vision of a Second Council of Jerusalem 123
• It is the Inverse of the First Council (Acts 15) 123
• Great Humility is Required 124
• The Elder Brothers Need to be Accepted 124
• The Messianic Jews have a Particular
    Role within the Body 124
• It will Bring Healing from the Wounds of Separation .. 125

continued......

.......continued
- An Ecumenical Earthquake 126
- Unity in Diversity & Unity Through Diversity 126
- Jerusalem will be the Centre 127
- There will be a Re-ordering of Christian Teaching 127
- To Prepare for the Second Coming 128
- The Realisation of the 'One New Man' 129
- The Last Miracle of Jesus before his Second Coming .. 129

ONE

WHY CARE ABOUT ISRAEL?

It is impossible to understand the Bible with its narrative about the plan that God has for mankind without understanding the role of Israel as a people and a Nation. The Jews have been at the centre of all that God does, beginning with the call of Abraham up to the book of Malachi at the end of the Old Testament; and they remained the centre throughout the period of the first Christian century recorded in the New Testament. However, it is not an exaggeration to say that the relationship between Jews and Gentiles within the Communion of Faith, since the coming of the Son of God, has been the most misunderstood in human history.

Our goal in these pages is to seek a more balanced, Biblical view of the Body of Jesus within God's plan of salvation. We try to offer a deeper understanding of how the Church should function according to God's plan; and how it will always remain in some way dysfunctional as long as one of the two essential components of the Church is missing. We look at the Scriptures, and history, to make an accurate analysis of the tragic situation we inherited from the past, which persists until today.

A JOKE WITH LOTS OF MEANING
One day, the Chief Rabbi of Jerusalem visited the Pope in

Rome. When he reached the Pope's office, the first thing he saw was a big red phone on the table. Soon he deduced that it was the 'hot-line' to speak to the Almighty. He did not think twice and said, 'Could I use your phone for a moment?' The Pope replied, 'Please be very careful; the long-distance calls from this phone are very expensive!' So, the Rabbi picked up the phone and started talking. He talked and talked and talked for a long time without any hurry. The Pope began to get nervous and looked repeatedly at the clock. Finally, the Rabbi hung up, thanked him and said that it had been a wonderful conversation. But the Pope was horrified because the bill for that conversation would certainly be very high.

A year later, the Pope was visiting the same Rabbi in Jerusalem and to his surprise; he also had a red phone. He thought, 'Oh, he took a long time on the phone in Rome, now I will call from his phone and do the same thing he did to me.' Thus, following the example of the Rabbi, the Pope also spoke on the phone for a long time. Nevertheless, the Rabbi was not the least bit nervous during the conversation. Finally, the Pope hung up and apologised: 'Rabbi, forgive me, I'm sorry for talking so long.' However, the Rabbi turned to him, smiled and said: 'Don't worry. From Jerusalem, talking to God is just a local call!'

THE JEWS – THE WORLD'S DESTINY

Marthe Robin (1902-1981), a famous French mystic, spent

much of her life paralysed, trapped in bed. Because of her spirituality and communion with God, many important Catholic leaders and a multitude of ordinary people sought her advice and prayers in her bedroom. This continued until her death, when she was almost 80 years old. While still young, in the 1920s, she had a vision in which she saw a young man whom she later identified as Adolf Hitler. In the vision, this young German stood in front of Satan wondering what he would have to do to gain importance, influence and even dominion over the earth. The devil replied to him, 'If you hand over to me all the Jews on the earth, I will give you dominion over the whole world.' Marthe understood from this vision:

1. Satan had found the ultimate way to block God's plans for salvation;

2. The key to doing so would involve eliminating the Jews from the world stage and history;

3. One day, a young German would sell his soul to become the instrument of extermination of the Jewish people.

This story reveals a very important truth. *From God's perspective, Israel is in the centre of everything of importance! All spiritual developments of global perspective are related to Israel. The God whom we serve will always be the 'God of Israel.'* We do not worship just the One and Only God Almighty – distanced from human history. We worship the God who appeared within man's history – as the God of Abraham, Isaac and Jacob. This is something very special and relevant. It is why Karl Barth, one of the major Lutheran theologians of the 20th century, is credited with the following quote: *'The question that most determines the future of the Church and how it operates will be determined by its relationship with Israel.'*

It is not really possible to understand what the Church is, let alone talk about the 'Messianic Jewish phenomenon' without first being deeply confronted with the fact of Israel´s election - **Israel as the Apple of God´s eye**.

The Church of the Gentiles will never reach the full measure of engagement with the plan of God on earth without understanding that it serves not just any God – but specifically the God of Israel. This has implications in all areas of our faith: in our theology and Christology, in our personal prayer life and our corporate worship, in our morals, in our evangelism, in the way we live out our family life in private and in the way that we are 'Church'.

THE MYSTERY OF ISRAEL'S ELECTION
'When the Most High gave the nations their inheritance, when he divided all mankind,... For the Lord´s portion is His people, Jacob his allotted inheritance. In a desert land he found him... he shielded him and cared for him, he guarded him as the apple of his eye (Dt 32:8ff).

Why Israel? Why did God choose this small, seemingly insignificant people group located in a tiny area between

Africa, Europe and Arabia? Why them and not us? We could easily become jealous! Is not that our thinking? Wouldn't it have been better if God had chosen us – our people, our nation? What about the Americans, the Brazilians, the Italians – or the Germans (as was the conviction of the Nazis)? Did God make a mistake?

It may even be natural to feel jealous of God's choice, but we would be ignoring the fact that God is completely sovereign when it comes to His choices. There is a non-negotiable, and perhaps incomprehensible, eternal decision of God: The election of Israel as His People. Whom do we question about His choice? He is the giver of life. He calls into being. He decides whom He chooses and whom He appoints for any specific purpose. There is no other way than to bow before this sovereign God, to accept whole-heartedly and with joy this election of Israel, and to acknowledge God's wisdom behind it.

We could speculate and suggest many reasons why God decided as He did: the location between the three continents; their semi-nomadic nature with its special religious tradition, which was open to a particular understanding of God's presence in the world. But such human explanations would not be sufficient. In the end, we have to accept that God chooses whom He chooses. And He chose this small ethnic group to be the *'apple of His eye'*. *'The Lord did not set his affection on you and choose you because you were more numerous than other peoples, for you were the fewest of all peoples.'* (Dt 7: 7) Israel is not better than the others, she has not more to give. Israel is just chosen!

The mystery is even deeper. He not only chose Israel out of all the other nations. In a sense, he even created Israel. He formed a people out of this old couple, Abraham and Sarah, when they received their son Isaac. Out of Abraham and his wife God created a nation for himself. For their offspring He gave them the land of Israel. And he created his people not just for his own pleasure but for the salvation of all the other nations.

Hand in hand with the election of Israel goes her calling. Israel is not chosen for her own benefit. God's people are called to be a servant to the nations, to serve in a priestly ministry and to become the mediator between God and the nations. This is the ongoing vocation of Israel - to be and to remain the main actor in salvation history. From this background of the 'Mystery of Israel' which corresponds to 'The Mystery of The Olive Tree' we get the correct understanding of the importance of the Messianic Jewish phenomenon.

But before we try to understand more about their calling we need to enter more deeply into this unique love of God for His People. We need some emotional understanding which may help us to agree with God´s decision deep down in our own hearts. Many who have gone through this deepening process have their own 'story' of coming into a significant relationship with Israel. Most of them speak about an overwhelming experience of being suddenly 'in love' with Israel. They are now able to identify personally with God's love for Israel, which is followed by a deep sympathy for her, a realisation of the value of what God has given to this nation, expressed in a desire to stand behind Israel, to bless her and to pray for Israel's well-being and good.

Believers who have gone through this process say that this path has opened their eyes to understand some of the special dignity God has granted to all members of the Jewish People; to the rich and the poor; to the impressive and the ugly; to the morally outstanding and to those who are great sinners. None of them has ever earned this dignity, rather it has been given to them as part of their ministry among the nations: to be a blessing. To recognise this particular dignity of the Jews has nothing to do with a 'Judeo-phile' emotion. It follows a deeper revelation that we all need to receive if we want to collaborate more successfully with God's ways of salvation.

'Now if you obey me fully and keep my covenant, then out of all nations you will be my treasured possession. Although the whole earth is mine, you will be for me a kingdom of priests and a holy nation.' (Ex 19:5)

'You are to be holy to me because I, the Lord, am holy, and I have set you apart from the nations to be my own.' (Lev 20:26)

God does not love Israel more than any other nation. A Jew is not more important in God's eyes than any other human being. Nevertheless, God needs to have this unique relationship with all who belong to His people, for the role of Israel has to be lived out by the Jews both collectively and individually. It is all about their vocation, since it's only because of this vocation that their election makes sense. In this dignity, Israel is called to be the Servant of the Lord (Is 42; Is 49; Is 50; Is 52 &53). This is true, independently of whether all Israel or each individual in Israel, is willing to do the will of God or not, or even understands it. The only important thing is what God has in mind for Israel and not what Israel has in mind for God (Ben Chorin).

For this role Israel had to be taken aside, out of the nations, to become a priestly nation, separate and different enough from the other nations to be able to live according to the will of God; to be the *'light to the nations'* (Is 49, 3; Lk 2:32). The centre of her vocation is to be a role model; an icon of how mankind could turn back to the order of God after individual and collective sin had destroyed His healthy image in the heart of every human being.

This vocation to be a role model is connected to the gift of the Land because the will of God has to be lived out in the context of society. This righteousness needs to be expressed in the form of a people living in a state.

A SECOND CONVERSION

As Gentile Christians we need a 'second conversion' - a

conversion to the God of Israel and to Israel as His people. To relate to God in a healthy way we need to understand this mystery and to accept Israel's role in God's plan. We need this conviction to be able to cooperate with God and His redemptive plan.

When we speak about a second conversion, we are not talking about our personal salvation, justification or eternal life. The first conversion happens when we recognise Jesus as the Lord of our life. This step is about forgiveness of sins and about the Spirit of God dwelling within us. His grace is enough to rescue us individually from sin and death. It is true that, if we are faithful to this first conversion, we lack absolutely nothing for our individual redemption. The problem is that most Christians only come to this first conversion as an individual experience between themselves and God. Many Christians never understand the role of the People of God. Too many are content with this 'vertical' relationship with God and focus solely on their own individual salvation.

To understand salvation in its fullness, we also need the horizontal dimension of our redemption. We need to be placed within the People of God, Israel and the Church. Man needs restoration, not only in his individual relationship with God, but also in the larger social and collective dimension. This horizontal dimension means being rightly placed within the People of God, called together to serve mankind as the People of God for the transformation of at least part of the 'world' into the Kingdom of God. For this second conversion, we need to understand the role of Israel.

We need to see the ultimate divine plan for all of us. Salvation involves the social dimension, the healing of all humanity, even the healing of all Creation around us. Jesus is not only Lord of our individual lives, but also the King of Israel and the King of Kings for the nations. For this role God chose Israel to be His people and to become the nucleus of healing for all peoples. There is need for God's relationship with this particular Nation, and for a certain form of relationship between Israel and the other nations, to bring about His Kingdom. Knowing about this is not an academic exercise but rather a receptive act which requires a new conversion through a widening of the heart. When we finally understand God's original intention, we will respect His choice and wholeheartedly welcome Israel.

Without embracing and cooperating with Israel, Christianity tries to bring about the healing of the world (tikkun olam) without the biblical foundation. When we neglect the Jewish roots of our Christian faith, Church life becomes in some way artificial. A special example of such a weakening of Christianity because of the denial of our Jewish roots is the situation of Christian denominations in the Middle East. For centuries, Christians in the Arab world have paid a high price to live out their faith in Christ. There are many vibrant churches in these regions.

Nevertheless, almost all those churches share the same problem. They usually deny their relationship with the Jews even though they sing the Jewish Psalms and read the Jewish Gospels. Because of a stronger identification with Arab national interests, they will not accept the fact that Israel is the *'apple of God's eye.'* Even though most of those churches have suffered for Christ in martyrdom, denying the Jewish roots of the Church has substantially weakened them in some aspects of their faith. Even though they think this denial provides protection against Islamic persecution, in fact, it hinders them from coming into their full identity – from taking on their role as bridge builders in this region. This makes them even more vulnerable to Islamic repression and terror.

My Personal Conversion to Israel

Before I go on with this theological reflection, I want to share my personal conversion story. My first encounter with God was at the age of seven. It was a privilege to be born in a Catholic family, where the emphasis was on family prayer and reading the Word of God together. My initial desire was to become a priest. At the age of twelve I lost my childlike faith because of a very severe crisis with my father. In the emotional vacuum that the crisis generated within me, and even as a kind of vindictive reaction, I attached myself to my maternal grandfather. He took the place of my father and started to exert a very strong influence on me. From him I received a very different worldview. This would not have been such a negative factor if not for a very serious detail – my grandfather was a fervent Nazi, a true disciple of Hitler, even though it was many years after the war.

During the years of World War II, my grandfather was serving in the National Socialist Party in a full-time position and was responsible for the administration of finances in our region. He was then ordered to take over the financial management of the Jewish extermination department in the region around Vienna. My grandfather was thrilled. This was his chance to make a great career. However, when he came to tell his wife about the order, my grandmother who was a fervent Catholic believer replied immediately and without hesitation, 'If you accept this position, I will divorce you.' Thank God, my grandfather loved his wife and considered keeping his marriage more important than advancing his career within the Nazi Party. As a result, the hands of my family were clean of Jewish blood.

As punishment for his decision, the Party sent my grandfather to serve as a simple soldier on the Russian front line of the war. My grandmother was taken to a psychiatric hospital. Despite having suffered so much at the hands of the Nazis, my grandfather kept his absolute fidelity to the ideals of Hitler even after the war. He continued to idolise Hitler. When I bonded with him as a young naïve boy of twelve, I was absorbing like a sponge all his demonic philosophy and German racist ideology with its aim to dominate the whole world.

I started to hate the Jews, convinced that they caused all the world's problems. I believed they were manipulating world politics, the economy and the media and that they were standing in the way of my German people becoming the first among the nations. Therefore, as Germans, we needed to eliminate the Jews. It was a terrible and sinful jealousy, which became a dangerous demonic power within me. As a boy, I experienced how much Hitler's Nazism was not just a system of political theory, but a real evil force. it began to poison my heart and transform me into another person. Without meaning to, I began to serve the devil's goals.

The exposure to my grandfather's influence lasted about three years. It was a short time, but enough to give me a 'brain-washing' and lead me to dive head-on into my grandfather's way of thinking.

By the grace of God, I had a new experience with Jesus at the age of 17 and found my way back to the Christian faith. This occurred during the meetings of an independent evangelical church. Shortly after, led by the Holy Spirit, I left the independent evangelical church and went back to my Catholic circles. This was not an easy decision. What was first done out of obedience to God, without understanding, turned out to be an important step towards my future ministry within the body of Christ. My wife and I, together with others, started an Ecumenical Christian community within the Catholic Charismatic Renewal Movement. I finished my theological studies, was ordained a permanent deacon in the Church and later even became the director of the deacons' seminary. Before long, I was acknowledged as one of the major revival leaders in our nation, especially known for my ongoing investment in Christian unity and reconciliation work between the various denominations.

However, there was something in me that had not changed. On the outside, I lived as a dedicated Christian. I knew how to worship, preach, and say all the right words. I taught Christian theology. I did these things with sincerity for I had had a real experience with God. *I was living one dimension of Christianity, but without the complete truth and without the second conversion.* Nevertheless, the demonic ideology and the hatred of the Jews remained a poison in my heart. Even though I occupied quite strategic leadership positions working for Christian unity in Austria, my relationship with Israel was still ambiguous. Although no-one knew about the attitude deep in my heart, it limited my freedom to minister. I didn't realise where it came from, but I was aware that something important was out of order in my life.

The year 1995 marked the 50th anniversary of the end of the War. Charismatic leaders in Austria organised a repentance march in commemoration of the Nazi sins committed against the Jews and the inability of Christians of that time to stand up against it. The route of the march started at the Hungarian border, going from there to Austria's most horrible concentration camp, Mauthausen. This 'March of Death' was forced on approximately 250,000 Jews and occurred during the last days of the War. Thus, to demonstrate repentance, the Christian leadership circle decided that, in an act of identification, we would have to take the same route that the Jews had taken fifty years before. I, being the president of this group, would obviously have to participate.

During the march, many wept, experienced feelings of sadness and spoke prayers of repentance. And there I was, among them! 'What am I doing here? I cannot relate to any of this', I thought to myself. They blew a shofar every five kilometres, and I felt as though my whole body was being consumed. It seemed that the piercing sound penetrated me from head to toe. It was as if God was knocking at the door of my heart. The inner feeling of torment grew so much that I thought I would go crazy. That sound was finally purifying my inner being, healing me and freeing me from the demonic force that still had access to my life.

Arriving at the concentration camp, I knew it was time to change. God's power was invading this reserved area of my life and, when I finally gave in, I cried for hours until all the demonic trash was out of me. It was a cry of deep cleansing and purification. Suddenly, my world changed. Even though I had been a believer for more than twenty years, from that moment on I began to see

Jesus in a different light. Now he was Jesus *the Jew*! I also looked at the apostles and recognised: 'that's Peter, the Jew; John, the Jew; Mary, the Jewess.' I came to see all the People of God in a Jewish light. I made the following prayer to God: 'As I was a curse to the Jewish people, from now on I want to be a blessing to them.' A few months later, God began to answer that prayer, using me to do just that.

I am sharing my experience here to make clear that there are two different forms of Christianity: one that tries to develop its divine mission without Israel, and another Christianity, still much smaller, but growing in the power of the Spirit, deeply rooted in its Jewish origins and open to maintaining unity and relationship with the Jewish people. That is why I am speaking about this second conversion. I believe that every Christian should go through it. It may be more traumatic, similar to my experience; or it may be a rather peaceful process that yields a deep change. But it needs to happen.

TWO

ALL BLESSINGS ARE MEDIATED THROUGH ISRAEL

EVERYTHING STARTED WITH ABRAHAM. The vocation of Abraham is the Biblical basis for this key role that Israel has in the divine plan of salvation. Genesis 12:1-3 refers to the call of Abraham and to God's promise to him as a permanent Covenant to all of his offspring.

The Lord said to Abram, '...*I will make you into a great nation, and I will bless you; I will make your name great, and you will be a blessing. I will bless those who bless you, and whoever curses you I will curse; and all peoples on earth will be blessed through you.*'

With this promise, God determined that all the great blessings of humanity would be, from that moment onward, related to Israel. This includes all 'salvation', all the healing and restoration of nations, even all the repair of Creation following the sinful history of exploitation. It is God's plan for the Hebrew Nation that it would become the 'mediator of salvation' for all other peoples of the Earth. God finally confirmed this to all the Israelites with the covenant on Mount Sinai (Exodus 19:5-6).

Did Israel fulfill its calling? The Scriptures show that, time after time, century after century, the people of the promise were not faithful. Israel's history is one of idolatry, murder and adultery, oppressing the poor, breaking the Law and ridiculing the covenant in every possible way. Rather than being a holy people, set aside for their priestly vocation, mediating between God and the nations, their desire was to be like the other nations. Unwilling to accept the dignity of the covenant, they refused to be different. When Israel forced Samuel, the prophet, to give them a king, as other nations, it was just another indication that Israel did not capture the uniqueness of its calling, but rather wanted to exchange its birth-right for material blessings and to determine its own way.

But God has bound himself, to the everlasting promise to Israel, for them to be the corporate source of blessing. He tried everything to bring Israel back to its ultimate purpose. He sent the prophets, He exercised varying degrees of discipline, and He urged them generation after generation to follow him. Even the punishment of the exiles only partially led to some kind of repentance and re-gathering. Even after the captivity, only a small remnant of the faithful in the Land was willing to turn with all their heart to God, their God of the covenant. Being surrounded by ignorance, this remnant people did the only possible thing: crying out for the coming of the Messiah to change the hardening of hearts.

However, when the Messiah, Yeshua of Nazareth, finally came, he was not coming the way they expected. Jesus did not assume a political role. He did not solve all of the Nation's problems, by defeating the Romans and leading Israel to become important again. No! Yeshua came to free His disciples from the tyranny of legalism and help them to fulfill the deepest meaning of Torah, at least in their own life. Instead of political revolution, He came to bring freedom to their hearts. Because He was not fulfilling their political, religious and eschatological expectations, most of the Jews rejected Him saying that He could not be the Messiah sent by God and so they crucified Him.

Jesus understands His messianic ministry as the fulfilment of Israel's role as a people. In Him, in His life and in His cross, everything that Israel was destined to accomplish corporately is becoming reality, a form of 'sacramental' reality. Initially sent only *'to the lost sheep of Israel'* (Matthew 15:24), Jesus tries to help them return to their role as a priestly nation, according to God's promise to Abraham. In the end, Jesus fulfilled the corporate mission as the suffering servant (Isaiah 53) exercising in His body the 'sacramental' representation on behalf of all of Israel.

THE JEWISH REMNANT
Only a small group of saints remained after the resurrection – the apostles, the relatives of Jesus and a few disciples. This remnant understood that the Messiah, rejected, crucified and resurrected was the One bringing salvation to Israel and to the world. They understood that it would be their priestly role as a remnant of 'believing Israel' to become the messengers of this salvation. As the 'New Israel' they should fulfill – for the sake of the nations – what Israel as a whole had failed to do.

Nevertheless, at first, they did not fully grasp how this worldwide vocation should be exercised. First, they preached the Gospel only to the Jews in Jerusalem and Judea. Then, they began to leave Jerusalem for Samaria and went further out still to the other nations, going from one synagogue to another. They preached to the Jews that the Messiah had come, differently than expected, but nevertheless, He was the fulfilment of parts of the promise. However, most of the Jews did not want to hear their message. With some exceptions in most of the synagogues, only a small number was willing to believe.

According to the word of Paul that salvation was *'first to the Jew, then to the Gentile'* (Romans 1:16), some of these apostles began to recognize that this atonement of the Messiah was not just for the Jewish people. They had seen some of the Gentiles thirsting for God much more than many Jews did. These Gentiles yearned for the freedom that they heard the Jewish Messiah had brought for His people. Some of them responded more readily to Jesus' message. So, the apostles concluded that this message was not only to the Jews, but also for all among the nations who seek God with a passionate heart. The healing that Jesus provided on the cross for Israel was meant for the Gentiles as well. (Romans 1:16)

Others among the apostles did not agree. It could not be that they had to share their Messiah with the other nations. They insisted – Israel is a separate and set aside people, a priestly nation, the only one that has access to God, and to His Messiah, and to His redemption. This access was, they believed, only for those born into the Sinai covenant, and those from the nations freely joining Israel as proselytes. For those it meant becoming a Jew by living under the complete

Law and all of its commandments. This faction of elders and apostles did not want to have anything to do with the Gentiles saved by Yeshua unless those Gentiles became Jewish proselytes first.

THE FIRST COUNCIL OF JERUSALEM

In the New Testament, we find many passages referring to this debate among the Jewish disciples of Jesus (Acts 15:1-35; Phil 3:1-4; Gal. 2:11-21).This conflict almost divided the new People of God. Paul's letter to the Galatians (Gal 2: 11-21) observes that there was strong disagreement between Peter and Paul over this issue. To resolve the differences, the apostles decided to hold a conference, later called by historians, the *'First Council of Jerusalem.'* At this *Council*, an important decision had to be made about the fundamental conflict concerning the nature of the People of God.

There were two main parties with opposing positions in this Council. The 'Jerusalem Party' or the 'Party of the Torah,' led by James the 'brother' of Jesus, who argued that no one is able to follow the Jewish Messiah without first becoming a Jew. In contrast, the 'Mission-Party' led by Paul and Barnabas, was convinced that, when the Holy Spirit touched the hearts of Gentiles, they were free to join the people of Israel without becoming Jews first. God had already sealed them with the power of the Spirit and the dignity of becoming sons and daughters of Israel. For Paul and Barnabas it was obvious: Gentiles who freely decided to follow the Jewish Messiah were not subject to first becoming Jews, being circumcised and obeying the Jewish Laws.

After many arguments at the Council, interestingly it was James, the leader of the 'Jerusalem Party,' who presented the solution. Being initially in favour of the Jewish Law for all, he changed his position and became convinced that it would not be according to the will of God to place an excessive burden on the Gentiles. For him it became clear that it was not right to force the Gentiles to keep the whole Law, when the Holy Spirit wanted the believers from the nations to live without this burden. James understood that it would be these Gentiles who would ultimately bring the good news into the cultures of the nations at the far ends of the earth. He submitted a proposal, which was accepted by the other apostles whereby the Gentiles were only required to follow a few laws which were necessary to keep the 'table fellowship' between Gentile believers and their Jewish brethren. James' proposal had only four criteria to be followed by Gentile Christians: '*to abstain from food polluted by idols, from sexual immorality, from the meat of strangled animals and from blood*' (Acts 15:20). Without fulfilling these four requirements, Jews and Gentile believers could never be part of the same congregation, or, among other things, take the Lord's Supper together.

With the end of the *First Council of Jerusalem* a new chapter began for the people of God. From that day on, the Body of the Messiah consisted of two components, one people – two distinct components. There was the Messianic-Jewish component, which in the New Testament is called '*the Ecclesia of the Circumcision*'(see Ephesians 2:11). And, there was the Gentile component, which was formed by all the non-Jewish believers from the nations. The Messianic component of the

Church continued to live a fully Jewish lifestyle. The Gentile component was free to express the Gospel according to the particular style of living of their respective nations, as long as this lifestyle was compatible with the Gospel of Jesus. There were Jewish and Gentile congregations, and there were many mixed congregations. Even though there were two different components, it was still one united people.

To gain a deeper understanding of the relationship between these two parts of the Body of Christ, we need to reflect on Romans 9-11. Interestingly enough, these three chapters are little known by the majority of Christians. Seldom is a sermon preached on this subject. What a pity! Not understanding these three chapters, and the theology behind them, means Gentile Christians miss an important truth: The only way for the Gentiles to fully participate in the redemptive plan of God is to be in harmony with the believing part of Israel.

Speaking about full participation, I am not referring to individual salvation. The Word is still valid: *'For it is with your heart that you believe and are justified, and it is with your mouth that you profess your faith and are saved.'* (Rom 10:10). This is without question. *I'm speaking about the ability of the Gentile believers to play a role in the collective salvation. Our entrance into salvation history was possible because we Gentiles were spiritually inserted into the House of Israel* (see Eph. 2:11-16). Salvation history in all its dimensions only unfolds as believing Jews and Gentiles maintain an ongoing collaboration for the sake of the Kingdom. The outcome of salvation history, as prophetically described in the Book of Revelation, shows that we will not see full salvation without the participation of believing Israel. *Here again we see it: the Jews are the bridge that connects the Gentiles to God* (e.g.Rev 4:4; 14:1-5; 21:9-14; see also: CCC No. 674).

UNDERSTANDING THE MYSTERY OF THE OLIVE TREE

To demonstrate this fact of the life-giving connection of the Gentile believers with Israel, Paul uses the analogy of the olive tree (Rom 11: 13-24).

- The roots and the trunk of the olive tree symbolise the Fathers, the covenants, the Torah, the promises, and even the Messiah Yeshua himself (Rom 9: 4-5) – what makes up the Nation of Israel at its best – into which the Gentiles have been grafted like *'wild'* olive branches (Rom 11: 13-24).

- According to this analogy, our full life in God as part of the People of God depends on being correctly connected to the trunk of the Jewish tree and its roots. We – the Gentile believers – are branches of this Olive Tree of Israel – grafted-in by the blood of the Jewish Messiah.

- The blood of the Messiah has made us become 'spiritual' members of the **'Commonwealth of Israel'**. We are part of the Jewish people in a spiritual sense. As Gentiles, we should live in deep unity with Israel, but we should not copy the Jews and their way of living. This means incorporation in a spiritual sense.

- According to Paul, many of the Jews at **that time** were dead parts of the tree, broken-off branches, which may be grafted in again later (Rom 11: 17, 23).

- The Gentiles only have a position in salvation history because we are part of God's People – and linked to Israel through the Jewish part of the Church (Rom 11). The full measure of the Gentile's participation in God's plan for salvation depends on their connection to their Jewish roots.
- The realisation of this link between the Gentile believers and Israel only functions well when the Messianic Jewish movement acts as the bridge between the Gentile Church and the Jewish people.

Gentiles are spiritually part of the Jewish people, nevertheless they are not Jews. The Apostle Paul opposed the view that the Gentiles should become Jews. We should live as Gentiles, not under the whole Jewish Law, but according to those parts in the Gospel where Jesus teaches the relevant parts of the Torah for all his disciples – like the 'Sermon on the Mount' (Matthew 5:1-7:29). This is nothing less than Jesus' radical actualisation and interpretation of the five books of Moses. Wearing a yarmulke (kippah), following Jewish customs, imposing Jewish culture on Gentiles is not what God intended. As Gentiles, we should not take from the Jews what is particularly theirs. We should not become like them, but we should relate to them in unity and harmony.

This relationship of the Gentile believers with all Israel is made possible and activated through the Messianic Jews, the believing remnant from Israel (Rom 11: 5,6). As Jewish believers, they are still part of all Israel. At the same time, as disciples of Yeshua they are also part of the Body of Christ. *In their double nature, they are the link between Israel and the Church. Without the Messianic Jewish part, the Gentile Church is amputated and doesn't have full access to the olive tree.*

If there is no Messianic Jewish part of the Church, our spiritual health as Gentiles is limited; the Gentile part of the Church is not connected with its Jewish roots in a 'living' form. Through the Messianic Jewish apostolic generation of the Early Church, the Gentiles have been grafted into the olive tree. By this the Gentiles became heirs to the blessings promised to Abraham (Romans 9:4-5; Galatians 3:6-14). Through the Messianic Jews of our day we need to be reconnected with this heritage in an actual way today. That is why Paul warns the Gentiles, *'do not consider yourself to be superior to those other branches. If you do, consider this: You do not support the root, but the root supports you.'*(Rom 11:18).

GENTILES DEPEND ON ISRAEL – ISRAEL DEPENDS ON THE GENTILES

Even if we have **not** realised this in our Christian and Church life so far, we Gentiles are dependent on Israel. Throughout the history of salvation, Israel has played and always will play the central role. This truth has its culmination in Jesus Himself. As the Son of God, He was manifested in life as a Jew; born a Jew from a Jewish mother; living as a Jew in the midst of Israel; dying as the King of the Jews; resurrected as a Jew and is seated at the right hand of the Father as a Jew. And this Jewish connection continued with the generation of the first disciples. It was no accident that most of the disciples in the early Church were Jews. With the first congregations in Jerusalem and Judea, God showed how He intended Israel to bless the world in a new and even deeper way. Believing the Gospel of the resurrected Messiah, they trained a Jewish remnant preaching the Jewish Gospel to the Gentiles of the nations.

For the fulfilment of salvation history, the Gentiles needed the Messianic Jews to become heirs of the Jewish Gospel. But without the witness of the Gentile believers the Jewish Gospel would never reach out to ends of the Earth. Without the Gentiles, the Messianic Jews would never fulfill this calling to enculturate the Jewish Gospel into the life-style of the nations. That is why, according to Ephesians 2:11-22, Jesus broke down this wall of separation between Jewish and Gentile believers so that they would be able to work together hand in hand. The blood of Christ brought near all who were far off. He made out of the two, one Church. He reconciled the two peoples into one Body (v. 14). By this act God potentially healed the torn apart mankind into One New Man. That is why God never intended to divide the Jewish part of the Church from the Gentile part of the Church. For Him there is only one Church composed of both peoples.

THREE

A History of Replacement

SOMETHING TERRIBLE HAPPENED right at the beginning of the Church's history. The Gentile believers in Jesus soon rejected God's divine purpose. For the Evil One it must have been clear, if this unity between Jews and Gentiles continued, his reign over mankind would finally be lost. Already a victory over evil and death had been won when Jesus died on the cross and rose again. However, as long as Satan could separate the message of redemption and reconciliation from the realisation of the One New Man, as long as the proclamation of this message is disconnected from the context of unity between Jews and Gentiles, Satan has influence and even control over individuals and religious institutions.

Although Satan has already been defeated, he still makes the world serve him as its master. The basis of him keeping the Earth under control of hatred, division and war is to confuse and impede the relationship between the Church and Israel. Since the One Church is the instrument of healing and restoration of humanity, a divided Church is massively handicapped to fulfill its ambassadorial purpose. The victory of Jesus on the cross is still valid, without the union of Jews and Gentiles, but in a way limited to the individual aspect of redemption. As long as Satan can prevent the concrete advancement of the Kingdom, he is satisfied. This seems a spiritual mystery. Jew and Gentile united and functioning together as the Church, the One New Man, healed from one fruit of the original fall, the division of mankind, leads to the ultimate victory of the Kingdom. It is this union which transforms the world into the Kingdom of God – making the victory of Jesus on the cross finally relevant and practical beyond the individual human experience of salvation. That is why Satan fought from the beginning, precisely to prevent this unity.

THE JEWS SEPARATE THEMSELVES FROM THE NAZARENES

This may seem an exaggeration. Could it really be that this division, in fact, is the key in the hands of Satan to close the door to the advancement of healing and restoration? I really believe so. Let's take a brief look at history to understand **better** how Satan has implemented his strategy by greatly damaging the relationship between the Gentile Church and the Messianic Jews.

In the year 66 A.D., about 40 years after the death of Jesus, the Jews protested against the Romans and unleashed a long and bloody war. The Romans invaded under the command of Titus, besieged the city of Jerusalem and then crushed the rebellion in 70 A.D. and, in doing so, destroyed the Temple. It was the fulfilment of the prophecies of Jesus in Matthew 24 and Luke 21.

Several decades later, around the year 132 A.D., the Jews began a second uprising. A man called Bar Kokhba led the rebellion.

He presented himself before the Jews as the promised Messiah and claimed an appointment by God which would be proved when he freed Judea from Roman oppression. Militarily unimportant as they were, the Jews were vigorous enough to protest against this mighty power. The Roman soldiers returned, this time under Emperor Hadrian, and devastated the entire city of Jerusalem. They expelled the Jews from the city and large parts of Eretz Israel. The Romans uprooted the Jews from the Land and left them stateless. By giving a new name to the province of Judea – Palestine ('land of the Philistines') – they declared the time of the Jews to be over. This second Exile of the Jews into the Diaspora was far-reaching and profound. They were scattered into all regions of the earth. Israel no longer existed as a nation.

As a result of these wars, the Jews began to hate the Romans and their collaborators. And, vice versa, the Romans hated the Jews and wanted to crush this 'small tribe' completely. Among all the provinces of the Empire, Judea had proved to be the most 'stubborn' one, always causing problems. Jews, in general, became 'persona non grata' within the Empire.

For Messianic Jews, the situation was even worse, they were in the crossfire. Both parties – the Jews and Romans – hated them. The Jewish side blamed the Messianic Jews for the defeat by the Romans. The Messianic Jews had refused to fight against Rome, convinced that this rebellion was not ordered by God, but was instead God's judgment against the Jewish people for their unbelief. So, the Messianic Jews were blamed as collaborators of the Romans and traitors. As a result, nationalistic Jews slaughtered many Messianic Jews. At the same time, the Messianic Movement was weakened from within. Instead of maintaining unity, they were separating themselves into groups of varying theological opinion. Some sects even abandoned the foundations of the apostolic beliefs of the early beginnings.

Around the year 92 A.D, after the destruction of the Temple, a synod was held in Jamna (Yavne), a city near Jaffa (now part of Tel Aviv) on the Mediterranean Sea. This synod brought together most of the leading Pharisaic rabbis of that time period, both from Israel and the Diaspora. The theme was: 'How could Judaism survive without a Temple?' Only two options were seen:

- either to continue with a wide variety of Jewish groups, which could quickly make them lose their identity as a people and therefore not survive the danger of assimilation under diaspora conditions;
- or to unite Judaism around a relatively rigid system of laws and regulations which excluded all dissident groups. This option was predominately directed against the Messianic Jews.

The second option was adopted. The synod ended with a declaration that the Messianic Jews, called 'The Nazarenes', would be removed from the people of Israel. From that time onward, this became the rule. If a Jew believes that Yeshua is the Messiah, he automatically ceases to be Jewish. This principle still prevails even today. If someone with Jewish blood wants to return to the Nation of Israel, the immigration authorities will always ask questions about their faith. If the applicant believes in Buddhism or even declares himself an atheist, this will not be a problem. But if the applicant confesses his faith in Jesus Christ, he will be prevented from entering the state of Israel as a Jewish citizen. With this exclusion from the Jewish people, the Messianic Jews have lost their homeland, their nationality, and their birthright to be regarded as part of the Jewish people.

THE FIRST DIVISION IN THE CHURCH

The Messianic Jews were sitting between a rock and a hard place! There was an anti-Jewish climate that had developed throughout the Roman Empire. On one hand, the Romans considered the Messianic Jews as a part of the Jewish people without any differentiation. Like all the other Jews, they had to be crushed and scattered throughout the world, never to cause problems again. On the other hand, they were even more dangerous than the traditional Jews as their faith in the Messiah pushed them automatically into opposition to the Roman Emperor and his almost God-like position.

Consequently, because the Messianic Jews actually were Jewish, it became dangerous for anyone to have any kind of a relationship with them. As a result, the Gentile Christians increasingly avoided mixing with 'these Messianic Jews.' The Gentile Christians already had enough problems with the Roman State as persecution of Christians was experienced in multiple ways. Avoiding the Jews eliminated at least one reason for persecution of Christians. As a result, the Gentile bishops failed to invite the Messianic Jewish bishops to their regional councils. This was crucial to the separation of the two parts. It was in those summoned meetings, during the first four centuries, that the Church synods decided about the common faith and the theology that supported it. They developed the key aspects of an emerging Christianity by interpreting the faith and heritage of the apostles and Jewish beginnings of the Church into Theology, Christology and Ecclesiology. And they did it without a Jewish presence. How could they decide about the Messianic Jewish heritage in a balanced way without Messianic leaders participating in this process? By the end of the third century the Messianic Jews were already being completely ignored.

The Church excluded lots of Jewish elements from its services, the liturgical calendar and the style of worship. They eliminated Jewish music and expunged from their teachings much of the vestige of Jewish influence. *It was a conscious and definitive separation made by the Church. They wanted to show to the public their complete separation from anything Jewish.* Around 250 A.D., outside of Judea, nearly all Messianic congregations ceased to exist. The few groups that remained lived secretly, without any outside influence, and, due to their isolation, many of them developed strange or even sectarian tendencies.

THE DRAMA OF REPLACEMENT THEOLOGY
All this pragmatic development called for substantial theological reasoning. Around the year 200 A.D., a new theological conviction began to sweep Gentile Christianity.

This theological foundation had to rationalise and justify that which was already happening. In later centuries, this theological system was called 'Supersessionism' or 'Replacement Theology.'

According to Replacement Theology, in his anger with the Jews for killing the Messiah on the cross, God revoked His covenant with Israel. Since they were no longer the covenant people, the Jews lost their birth right and, as a people, were deprived of divine grace. No longer the Chosen People, they had to remain in a state of collective sin under condemnation from God.

In their place, there was a new 'Chosen People,' the Church, seen as the 'New Israel' – replacing the 'Israel of the flesh'. This meant that all the blessings and promises God had made to Israel in the Scriptures (as a result, from this time onward called 'Old Testament') now belonged to the Gentile Church. And all the curses coming upon Israel belonged to the Jewish people. Suddenly, the Jews were transformed into enemies of God, enemies of mankind and enemies of the Church.

This theology was not the product of some extreme outsiders but rather, the conviction of most of the best theologians of the time, known as the Church Fathers, both in the Western and in the Eastern part of the Empire. As a result, Replacement Theology became the leading ideology of both the Catholic as well as the Eastern-Orthodox and the Old Oriental world. Here are some examples:

The **Letter to Barnabas** was written around the year 100 A.D. Although not officially part of the Bible, it was understood to be inspired by God as an important document of the apostolic time. Written by an unknown author, probably a disciple of or at least someone close to the apostles, the letter speaks about the loss of the Jewish birth right and, because they had killed the Messiah, the Jews were excluded from the people of God and the Church.

Ireneaeus of Lyon, (135 – 202 A.D.), according to some a disciple of John, was one of the most important theologians of his time. Even though he preserved, within his dogmatic writings, the Jewish heritage of the Church of Asia Minor he, nevertheless, strongly emphasised that Christians should avoid any kind of relationship with Jews in order to prevent confusion in their faith. He wanted the Church to be cleansed from all Jewish elements.

Origen, (+ 254 A.D.), one of the most famous Fathers of the Eastern Church, introduced the terminology of 'Ancient Israel' and 'New Israel.' For him, the 'Old Israel' was of the 'flesh' as the 'New Israel' was born of the Spirit. As Christians belonged to the New Israel and did not need the Jewish blood; it is enough to be baptised in water since the Spirit then came and took the place of the blood.

Ambrose, (337 – 397 A.D.), the famous bishop of Milan, Italy, exercised much influence on Augustine and his teaching. For him, it was not enough to affirm that the Jews were no longer a part of the Church, but the Church must also exert the judgment of God upon them. This should be the role of the Church. Even though Ambrose was well known as a holy man and a great leader of the Church, in regard to the Jewish issue, he developed a certain blindness. Against the Emperor, he publicly defended a bishop in the East, who in his anger against the Jews even took a torch and led a Gentile mob to Jewish homes to burn them down. Ambrose was convinced that the more suffering imposed on the Jews, the humbler they would become and the more open to the Gospel of Jesus.

Augustine, (354 – 430 A.D.), bishop of Hippo Regio in Algeria, was one of the most influential Church Fathers within Western Christianity. For him it was clear: Christians were not allowed to kill Jews. However, God had to keep the Jews alive to use them as a negative example of divine judgment on a nation that abandons Him. Thus, Christians felt authorised to persecute the Jews, but not kill them.

John Chrysostom, (344 or 355 – 407 A.D.), patriarch of Constantinople, was the most venerated theologian of the Byzantine Church. He was called 'Chrysostom' – 'The Golden Mouth' – because of his outstanding teaching gift. Thousands of people surrendered their lives to Christ when he preached the gospel. However, he hated Jews and preached eight famous sermons full of venom against them. He warned his listeners to have nothing to do with the Jews, neither in their daily contact, nor by visiting their synagogues or participating in religious occasions. For him, it was necessary that Christians avoid any kind of contact with Jews, in order not to get 'infected with the Jewish disease.'

All of these theologians had great revelations concerning the Kingdom. But, concerning the role of the Jews in God's plan for salvation, they were more or less blind. The devil fomented it, knowing that as long as Christians do not fail to understand the 'mystery of Israel', he would remain dominant in the world. The same blindness is found among Christians today. Very often individuals, who are very dedicated to God, also have a blind spot when it comes to the Jewish issue.

From Replacement Theology to Anti-Semitic Politics

The Replacement Theology of the Church Fathers established principles, which guided Christian practice and politics for centuries. A Church and state legislation against the Jews followed. From the third century onward, a systematic 'cleansing' of the Church from all its Jewish heritage began. From synod to synod, the legislation became stricter to make sure that nothing of Jewish life remained.

Emperor Constantine, who stopped all Christian persecution and began to make use of the Christian Church as a main unification factor for the Roman Empire, forced all the Gentile bishops at the *First Council of Nicea* (325 A.D.) to 'cleanse' the Church from all things Jewish. With this same intention, he ordered (321 A.D.) Sunday instead of Shabbat (Saturday) as the holy day of the week and changed the dates for Easter so that its relationship with Passover would be lost.

The regional **Synod of Elvira/Spain** (306 A.D.) had already banned every interaction in private homes between Christians and Jews. For the first time, marriage between a Christian and a Jew was forbidden.

In 365 A.D. the **Synod of Laodicea** ordered all Christians who still kept Shabbat in their private homes were to be publicly excommunicated from the Church and, in some cases, even sentenced to death.

At the **Council of Chalcedon** (451 A.D.), the prohibition of marriages between Christians and a Jewish partner became a Church-wide regulation. Every Jew who was baptised, had to distance himself publicly from all of his Jewish family and heritage, and had to declare that he no longer belonged to the People of Israel. The Church authorities were even allowed to take away children from their Jewish families to be raised in a monastery as good Christians!

In 438 A.D., **Emperor Theodosius II** legalised the systematic transformation of Jewish synagogues into Christian church buildings.

From the **II Council of Nicea** (787 A.D.) onward, there began a terrible persecution of those baptised Jews who, in the privacy of their homes, continued to keep the Shabbat, to circumcise their children, and to live according to the Law of Moses.

Additionally, all this stigmatisation of the Jews led to a growing hatred against the Jews among uneducated mobs. According to the teaching of Augustine, even though the

Church normally did not allow Jews to be killed, in most cases, the bishops were not able to protect against the mob. In many situations, the bishops even sympathised with the uproar of the Christian masses as they mobilised on the streets against the Jews. Jews had become the enemies of Christ, the enemies of the Church, the enemies of everybody.

Their synagogues were burned. Their civil rights were denied. They needed to hide and live in isolated ghettos. In the Middle Ages, the Jews suffered under organised persecution and killings. During the crusades and in the following centuries, they were stripped of their goods, threatened and murdered in pogroms. When the Jews finally fled to Eastern Europe to find a more peaceful place on the earth – they eventually became victims of the Cossack-pogroms in the 17th and 19th century, primarily in Poland and Russia. All this being done in the name of Jesus.

There were more than 600,000 Jews in Spain and Portugal before 1492, when they were expelled from their respective countries or forced to convert to Christianity. The Jews who were forced to convert and be baptised were called Marranos. Most lived a double life. Acting as Catholics outwardly, they remained Jews in the privacy of their homes. Terrorised by the Holy Inquisition, they fled in their thousands to the colonies of the Americas in hope of freedom. But the Inquisition followed them to South America and the persecution continued there. Based on the Nicene decision, the Inquisition forced the new converts to deny any link with Judaism. A system of control was established: their neighbours watched them, everything was observed – what they kept in the barn, what they did during the time of Easter, if they dressed differently during Shabbat. If Jewish practice was identified, those lawbreakers were imprisoned, tortured, and even killed.

Thus, the Jews had experienced a long and uninterrupted history of alienation and persecution. *The ultimate consequence of the belief in and practice of Replacement Theology was the Holocaust of the Nazis.* Even though believing Christians have not been the perpetrators of the Shoah, the Christians were the ones who paved the way for this with hundreds of years of anti-Jewish teaching and propaganda. The Nazis were able to build their concentration camps on the pillars of Christian Anti-Judaism.

There is a possibility that Evangelicals today think this is a Catholic problem that does not concern them. Often, Evangelicals consider themselves free of this burden of sinful history because of their having broken off from Catholics and started something new. Therefore, they believe they are freed from any responsibility for the historical persecution of the Jews. However, it is not that simple.

Anti-Jewish ideology is also found in almost all streams of Protestantism, beginning with **Martin Luther** (1483-1546) and his anti-Semitic approach during the later years of his ministry. Frustrated about the small number of converted Jews after years of biblical preaching and Reformation he finally ordered the persecution of Jews and justified such atrocities in his sermons and writings, which influenced future Protestant generations. Beyond that, the poison of Replacement Theology is still working in many protestant denominations. They often follow a particular understanding of 'supersessionism' which means that there were certain periods ('dispensations') when the Jews had and/or will have to play a role in salvation history. But since the cross and the resurrection of Christ and the 'Grace-teaching' of Paul there is no role left for Israel in salvation history for the Gentiles. Consequently, the Church has no connection to Israel and/or to the Messianic Jews. In many cases, the sins of the Catholic Church were inherited by Protestant denominations and produced tragic fruit.

THE END OF MESSIANIC JUDAISM – THE JEWISH PART OF THE CHURCH

In this Replacement climate, it was no longer possible to believe in Christ and remain a Jew at the same time. A Jew who believed in Yeshua had to deny all his Jewishness. *Replacement Theology, therefore, brought two very tragic consequences: The **first** was the persecution of the Jews in general. The **second** consequence was the extinction of the Messianic Jewish presence in the Church.*

This extinction was catastrophic, not only for the Jewish part of the Church, but also for the Gentile part. As a result of this loss, the Gentile Church became disoriented and incomplete. The separation between Jews and Gentiles was the Church's first division. Numerous other divisions followed. This separation worked like a virus and contaminated the Church. It was perpetuated in every division according to the model of Replacement Theology. Even though it may not be so apparent at first sight – this replacement strategy is a fundamental characteristic operating within every division.

There are more than 30,000 different denominations – and in some way all of them believe about themselves that they are 'the true Church.' There is always a 'new' Church – better equipped to be 'the true Church of Christ'. Even for those who have separated themselves just recently and have established themselves – they will not keep their place as the One True Church for long. The process of replacement remains the same. A dissenting group, through the eyes of this bias, suddenly sees the Church they have separated from as not being worthy to continue to be the Church of Christ anymore. A 'younger' church takes the place of the 'older' one and declares itself as the true Church. As 'the new people of God', they replace the former. This will only last until there is another group that comes claiming that they know God even better, have a better worship, better teaching and have more of a right to occupy the position of God's representatives. This Replacement Cycle has repeated itself many times right up to today.

These divisions result from the structural sin that we inherited when we separated from our Jewish roots. The loss of the Jewish component not only caused divisions, but also produced many other negative consequences. If it is true that we are now part of the 'commonwealth of Israel,' and if it is true that our identity as Gentile Christians lies in the fact that we have been grafted into the Olive Tree, Replacement Theology has robbed us of our foundation.

A LIMITED ABILITY TO INTERPRET THE HEBREW SCRIPTURES

With the loss of the Jewish part of the Church, the Gentile Church also lost its natural ability to comprehend the heritage all believers have in Abraham. The Church of the nations in some ways lost its Jewish mindset. How can we read the Hebrew Scriptures if we are not looking through a Hebrew lens? Without understanding the original Jewish mentality, we are partially blind and we are tempted to interpret the Scriptures from a Gentile perspective.

Jerome (born 347 A.D. in Croatia, died 420 A.D. in Bethlehem), one of the Latin Church Fathers, knew about this hindrance. He followed his life's vocation to translate the Bible into Latin correctly by moving to the Holy Land and spending almost 20 years of his life studying with a Jewish rabbi. However, most theologians lacked this understanding.

Instead of the Jewish mindset, theologians replaced the loss by making use of other ways of thinking and different philosophical interpretations of the world. They used the Greek mindset, the mindset of the Romans and later the mindset of the German tribes in Europe. It could be said that this substitution is continued by many Churches of today when their teaching is mostly reflecting modern philosophy or even today´s lifestyle.

The lack of the Hebrew mindset resulted in misunderstanding and misinterpretation of the Hebrew Scriptures of both Testaments. This is because, although the New Testament

Scriptures were written in Greek, the original text was construed according to the Hebrew worldview of its authors. In the following centuries, this fact provoked endless debates between theologians. Many theologians claimed that they had the right key to the only possible interpretation. But who could be the judge that their interpretation was authentic? This fight over the right understanding became endless, especially after the Reformation and the founding of every new stream within Protestantism. As a consequence, many divisions within the Church occurred because each stream had a different mindset when it came to interpreting the Scriptures.

Like Karl Barth, (1886-1968), other theologians of the 20th century stated that the Jewish issue is at the heart of many of the ecumenical problems we face. Because the extinction of the Jewish part of the Church has separated the Church from its unifying Jewish roots, each denomination claims for itself the authentic Hebrew understanding. In reality, every Church has in some way its own subjective interpretation. How could anyone other than the Messianic Jews authentically say what the Jewish prophets, the Jewish Jesus and the Jewish apostles really meant? Therefore, there remains this thesis: *Unless this first division is addressed and healed, all the efforts to foster unity in the divided Body of Christ will continue to be frustrated.*

The terrible divisions of the Christian Church have not overcome the God-given glory. The Church is still a divine work of diversity, perseverance and faithfulness. She has kept the faith in Jesus over the centuries. Her testimony to the triune God is real. The Holy Spirit has been acting continuously within her throughout history. But all this is still incomplete and unable to meet the ultimate, great goal of God.

Without Christian unity the world will not believe (Jn 13: 35; 17: 21). But all our efforts on behalf of Christian unity will necessarily be weak and powerless as we will never achieve full unity in the Body of Christ without the cure for this first division.

The difficulty, however, is that we are not able to produce this healing just among the Christian denominations. This first division can be healed only if our Jewish partner 'returns.' But this Messianic Jewish partner - as a distinguishable partner - has disappeared since the beginning of the 4th century. During most of the seventeen centuries since then, we have been without them.

And, we are not too worried about it! We are hardly aware of their absence. And, we perceive ourselves as doing well and are comfortable with our current state.

However, Jesus will not return to earth until the Bride is restored to her fullness. The Body of Christ needs to be united, Jews and Gentiles unified into the One New Man. The heavens will retain Jesus until we have finished this work of reconciliation. We are now living in a time of grace that can bring about this unity. Our God is giving us hope to bring history to its consummation, completing all that remains for Jesus to return as Bridegroom.

If there is no resurrection of the Messianic Jewish believers, we can do our best, but it will not be enough. Without the Messianic Jews, we will not see the complete healing of the Body of Christ. We need the restoration of this Messianic Jewish part of the Body of Christ to enable this essential healing from all the divisions that are debilitating us. Only God can perform this miracle of resurrection.

FOUR

THE MIRACLE OF RESURRECTION THE MESSIANIC JEWS OF TODAY

ONE DAY, THE EMPEROR OF PRUSSIA, Frederick II, the Great (1712-86), an agnostic disciple of the Enlightenment movement, was discussing with his personal physician all kinds of problems related to the late 18th century. Finally, he confronted the doctor with the frank question, 'Is there any substantial reasoning for the existence of a personal God?' The physician replied, without thinking for too long, 'The Jews, my king, the Jews!'

FOUR RABBIS AND ONE PURPOSE

During approximately 1,400 years, between the 4th and 18th centuries, there was not as far as we know a Messianic Jewish body on earth. Suddenly, in the late 17th century, in a very sovereign and supernatural way, the Holy Spirit began to bring back the Messianic Jews. They resurfaced from the dead!

The first event that we know about happened in a small town in southern Poland, Pinczow (near Krakow), around the year 1680. Four well-known Rabbis – Rabbi Krokeffer and Rabbi Sender, both from what is now the Czech Republic and Rabbi Chaija Chajon from Turkey met with the Chief Rabbi from Pinczow, interestingly called among his people, 'Rabbi Megalleh Amukkoth' (the one who discovers secrets). As it was told in the documents later found in the Archives of Herrenhut the three rabbis who lived outside of Poland, were individually led by the Holy Spirit to come to this small town of Pinczow, to meet with their colleagues. They did not meet on just any day, but on the particular day of 'Tisha B'Av,' the Jewish day of fasting and mourning over the destruction of the Temple.

As they met, they discovered they shared the same sentiment. Deeply frustrated with the situation of the Jewish people, all four desired that God might bring a change. The Jews of their time were highly discouraged. Pogroms, like the one under the Ukrainian Cossack leader Bohdan Khmeinytsky, when 100,000 Jews were killed at one time, had terrified them. There was a great longing for the Messiah to come, and many were too easily persuaded, following everyone announcing himself as the expected Messiah. One of them was the well-known Sabbatai Zvi, who announced in 1665 a revelation that the following year would begin the Messianic Age and the establishment of the New World. Great was the distress when nothing happened a year later.

Others had already lost all their hope in Biblical prophecy, and they solved their frustration by giving up their Jewish lifestyle and assimilating into Gentile society. But this Gentile society in 'Post - 30 Years War – Europe' was not open to integrating them. The confusion among the Jews in Europe grew even more. The four Rabbis desired a new direction for their people.

In the course of their meetings, the four became overwhelmed by the presence of the Holy Spirit. After intensive studies of the Scriptures, especially the books of the prophets, comparing

THE MIRACLE OF RESURRECTION

them with the Christian New Testament, the veil fell from their eyes. They could see that lots of Old Testament prophecies were fulfilled in the person of Jesus Christ. They then understood that Yeshua of Nazareth is the Messiah of Israel and the Saviour of mankind.

According to their revelation, the four Rabbis began baptising each other in the *mikvah* of the house in Pinczow in the name of the Father, the Son and the Holy Spirit (under the Hebrew words, 'HaShem HaAv, HaBen VeHaRuach HaKodesh!'). Out of the Scriptures, they clearly saw that the Kingdom of God would be revealed soon. But before this could happen, Israel would have to convert to its Messiah and would form a 'Kahal,' a congregation of its own, parallel to the Kahal of the Gentiles. It was the Rabbis' conviction that through this recognition of Yeshua as their Messiah, Israel was no longer the enemy of Christ but instead, 'His people.' Now all nations on the earth would come to faith. On this night, the Messianic Jewish part of the Church experienced its secret resurrection.

The four Rabbis shared two convictions. It was clear to them they should not join any Gentile Christian church. If they did join a Christian church, they would cease to be Jews. As authentic Jews they wanted to preach in secret their faith among close friends. And so they did, and many were baptised.

The other conviction was that they wanted to be Jews and to remain in their Jewish culture, still going to the synagogue and living under the Law. But it was absolutely impossible to share their convictions publicly with other Jews. They knew that if they spoke about this truth, they would be excluded from their people or even killed. Although all of them were well known and respected rabbis in their circles, the time was not yet ripe. So, they decided to live their faith in secret.

Each began to form a clandestine cell of Jews who believed in the Messiah. They also wrote letters about their experience to friends living in different parts of Europe between London and Constantinople. Small groups were emerging in people's homes. Thus began a 'hidden' network of Jews who believed in Jesus. All these activities were kept secret because, if they had become public knowledge, the Jewish authorities would have quenched the movement.

Approximately 60 years later, a German count, Nicolaus Ludwig von Zinzendorf (1700-1760), became the first Gentile protector of this secret Messianic movement. Since his youth, he had been a man dedicated to Christian unity. Throughout his whole life he worked hard to reconcile Christian groups in Germany, France and wherever he had influence. As the founder of the Moravian movement, which was the first 'ecumenical community' in history, he became one of the pioneers of spiritual ecumenism.

In the year 1742, Zinzendorf understood that all his efforts for Christian reconciliation would be in vain if the first division of the Church – the split between Jews and Gentiles – was not addressed and healed. Therefore, when he heard of this underground network of Messianic Jews, Zinzendorf understood that God had again raised up the Jewish part of the Church. With the influence he had, he felt a responsibility to help the Jews and Gentiles unite.

Following this basic decision, he sent one his closest co-workers, Samuel Lieberkühn to Amsterdam to begin a new form of evangelism among the Jews of this city. He wanted Jews no longer to be baptised into the conditions of a Christian denomination. He wanted Lieberkühn to teach those Jews willing to follow Jesus as their Jewish Messiah to form their own Messianic Jewish congregations which Zinzendorf called 'Judenkille' (according to the Hebrew word for 'Kehila'). It began as a parallel experiment not only in Amsterdam but also in Herrenhut, Germany. It was the first time since the fourth century that baptised Jews were invited to continue their Jewish lifestyle, express their faith in Jesus in Jewish terms and at the same time have complete communion with their Gentile brothers and sisters in the Church. This was a big move. But with the death of the duke, this experiment of uniting Jews and Gentiles died. Again, the time was not yet ripe. However, his vision and his ideals did not disappear.

The Origin of the Modern Messianic Jewish Movement

It took another 200 years for Zinzendorf's vision to bear full fruit. In the beginning of the 19th century many Christians had suffered the terrible experience of Napoleon invading Europe with overwhelming power, which felt something like an Antichrist experience. As a result, many Protestant groups were awakened to take an interest in the future of Israel.

By studying the Scriptures, they understood that there would never be an eschatological consummation of God's plan and all prophecy without the return of the Jews to their homeland. So, in order to hasten the Second Coming of Christ, many Protestant congregations (mainly in Britain, the United States and Germany) began to take great interest in inviting Jews to become followers of Christ.

Until then, Jews who accepted Jesus as their Messiah had to give up all Jewish elements in their lifestyle. Now, for the first time, these Jewish believers in Jesus were allowed to continue living as Jews. Many congregations among the Anglicans, Baptists, and other denominations helped to develop what was called the **'Christian Hebrew Movement.'** Jews, who accepted Yeshua as their Messiah, formed Hebrew groups inside and under the umbrella of Gentile Christian churches. This was a radical missionary concept for that era. Though helpful for the moment, it was not a long-term solution because these 'Hebrew Christian congregations' still remained under the control and 'guardianship' of Gentile churches.

'The Church's Ministry Among Jewish People'(CMJ), formerly called 'The London Jews Society' and also the 'London Society for Promoting Christianity Amongst the Jews', and later on the 'Church Missions to Jews' is an Anglican example of this kind of missionary society founded in 1809. The society began in the early 19th century, when leading evangelical Anglicans, including members of the influential 'Clapham Sect' such as William Wilberforce, and Charles Simeon, decided that there was an unmet need to promote Christianity among the Jews.

In 1809 they formed the 'London Society for Promoting Christianity Amongst the Jews'. The agenda was:

- Declaring the Messiahship of Jesus to the Jew first and also to the non-Jew
- Endeavouring to teach the Church its Jewish roots
- Encouraging the physical restoration of the Jewish people to Eretz Israel and forming an independent state in the Holy Land, decades before Zionism began as a movement
- Encouraging the Hebrew Christian/Messianic Jewish movement
- Engaging in pro-Israel advocacy

The society's work began among the poor Jewish immigrants, with a centre in the East End of London, and soon spread to Europe, South America, Africa and Palestine. In 1813, a Hebrew-Christian congregation called *'Benei Abraham'* (Children of Abraham) started meeting at the chapel in Palestine Place, East London. This was the first recorded assembly of Jewish believers in Jesus and the forerunner of today's Messianic Jewish congregations.

'The London Jews Society' was the first such society to work on a global basis. In 1836, two missionaries were sent to Jerusalem: Dr. Albert Gerstmann, a physician, and Melville Bergheim, a pharmacist, who opened a clinic that provided free medical services.

In its heyday, the society had over 250 missionaries. It

supported the creation of the combined Anglican and Lutheran Bishopric in Jerusalem in 1841, and the first incumbent was one of its workers, Michael Solomon Alexander, a former Jewish Rabbi. The society was active in the establishment of 'Christ Church', Jerusalem, the oldest Protestant church in the Middle East, completed in 1849, which still is owned by CMJ and not under the control of the Anglican Church. At the time of the First World War the society was described as the oldest and best organised of its type, and had auxiliary societies in 52 countries in Europe, Asia and Africa. About 5,000 Jews have been baptised by the society since its foundation.

A next step happened in Moldova, a region belonging to Russia in the late 19th century. A Jewish merchant named **Joseph Rabinowitz**, who lived in Kishinev, Moldova, was very concerned about the growing anti-Semitism found throughout the entire region. So, he began helping young Jews to emigrate from Russia to Palestine to escape persecution. For a long time, the Jews in Moldova lived under a lot of pressure, with no prospect of a better future. This was mainly because the Orthodox Church, in partnership with the Tsarist state, was extremely anti-Semitic.

During one of his regular trips to Jerusalem, while walking on the Mount of Olives one day, Rabinowitz had a strong religious experience. He saw Jesus as a Jew coming towards him, saying: 'I am the One whom you seek; I am the solution to your problem.' After this experience, Rabinowitz was convinced that Yeshua was the Messiah and Saviour. From that moment on, his life changed. He decided to cease working so hard to bring Jews to Palestine, but instead, to invest all his energy and resources on Jewish evangelism in Moldova to win them to the Messiah. Those who were saved, in his hometown of Kishinev, formed the first independent congregation of Messianic Jews since the first centuries. He insisted that his congregation was not affiliated with any Christian church. This marked the birth of the completely independent Messianic Jewish Movement in the modern era.

Though a single experiment, the concept was already launched. The principle was to form Messianic Jewish congregations that were independent from Christian denominations. Although they did not have an institutional relationship with Gentile churches, they were now linked to them in a much deeper sense: as free partners.

However, it still took about 70 years more until the Messianic Movement experienced a significant breakthrough. The Lord still needed to prepare the world, and the Church, to understand that they needed to make room for the Jews in general and for this Messianic Movement in particular. This period was the worst time in the history of Judaism, as anti-Semitism reached its climax during the Nazi rule in Europe.

The Horror of the Holocaust Opened a Window of Unique Opportunity

At the end of World War II, six million Jews had been killed. All Jews, and the whole world with them, were in shock. As a consequence, a small window in time was open – a unique chance for an **independent State of Israel**. Under the pressure of sorrow over the genocide against the Jews by the Nazi regime and the inability of the free world to hinder this horrible mass murder, the United Nations took action. In November 1947 a majority of 33 states voted for the creation of an independent Jewish State. On the 14th May 1948, Ben Gurion, Israel's first Prime Minister, announced the creation of this sovereign State of Israel. Even though Israel had to fight for its existence right from the next day onwards in the War of Independence, this event changed the perspective of all the Jews in the world and gave them hope for the future.

David against Goliath

Thus, in 1948 when Israel was established, many Jews recognised Yeshua as the Messiah. Many, who were already secret followers of Jesus, decided to make their faith public, both in Israel and in many places, both in America and Europe, so a great start was made. The momentum of Messianic growth was even stronger after the Six Day War in June of 1967. The new born State of Israel was in real danger of extinction when all the Arab nations, with their military power, tried to annihilate the Jewish presence, and to expel all Jews from the region. As in the first War of Independence in 1948, Arab tanks came again from all sides in June of 1967, and again, an unexpected miracle happened. 'Little David' had victory over the great 'Goliath'. All the Egyptian aircraft were destroyed on the ground in one day. The battle against tanks from Syria on the Golan Mountains in the north of Israel was also successful, although with many losses. The large amount of money invested by Saudi Arabia in the war was totally wasted.

The culmination of the war came when the Jews re-took the Old City of Jerusalem from Jordanian domination. The Roman emperor Hadrian, in 135 A.D., officially changed the name of the Jewish Homeland from Israel to Palestine, and decreed that the Jews would never again return, either to own or rule Jerusalem or any part of the Land of Israel. But in 1967, the Jews entered the historic city after decades of absence, prayed at the Wailing Wall and shortly after made Jerusalem their capital. It is hard to describe the kind of hope among the Jews that followed this event. For them, Old Testament prophecies were being fulfilled right before their eyes.

All Jews around the world were greatly motivated by this victory. The war lasted only six days and, on the seventh day, the soldiers celebrated the Sabbath. The news went around the world, and everyone wondered: *'How could such a thing have happened?'* This event made the Jews feel extremely blessed and proud. For them it was a clear sign: God had not abandoned them. As difficult as it may sound – to many Jews, it seemed that the six million Jews who had died in the Holocaust had not given their lives in vain.

Old Testament prophecies fulfilled

There were important Old Testament prophetic lines about Israel, four now seemed to have been fulfilled:
   (1) The Jews will possess the Land of Israel again as their own independent State (Amos 9:11-15);
   (2) The Jews will return to the Land, coming from the four corners of the earth – north, south, east and west (Isaiah 43:5-6);

(3) The arid desert land will become a huge green garden. In fact, today Israel is a lush green garden, while many of the countries around it are true deserts (Isaiah 35:1-2; 41:18-20);
(4) Before the end times, Jerusalem will be freed from the dominion of the Gentiles and will be the capital of Israel (Zechariah 1:17; 2:4; 12:1-9).

In 1948, there were about one and a half million Jews in Israel. By the end of the Six Day War in 1967, the number was growing to about five million. Constant waves of Aliyah (the immigration of Jews from the Diaspora to the land) ever since have brought thousands and thousands of Jewish immigrants into Israel. They came from all parts of the world, including Ethiopia and even countries such as India. After 1989 one million came from Russia alone, after Soviet communism had broken down. Today (2018) Israel has more than 8 million inhabitants of whom over 7 million are Jewish.

Before 1967, Jerusalem was a divided city – the Jewish section in the newer part of Jerusalem, and the Jordanian section in the eastern part. After the war, Israel declared Jerusalem its everlasting capital. Even though this decision ignored all the international protests that followed this significant political act, the leaders of Israel understood this to be in obedience to the prophecies of old. One of the reasons why all the peace negotiations, being attempted today between Palestinians and the Jewish State, have failed is because, for most Jews in Israel, Jerusalem is not negotiable.

When people see the old pictures of Palestine, at the beginning of the 20th century, most cities are small and devastated and the area around is rather treeless with mountains and a desert-like landscape. What a difference today! Usually, when tourists arrive in the Middle East, no matter in which country – Syria, Jordan, Egypt and even parts of Lebanon – dry land dominates the topography. Amid this immense aridity, the land of the Jews (except the Negev) is a small and green garden, with lush trees, huge fields of flowers and orchards laden with fruit.

But there is another prophetic line still waiting: The people of Israel, before the final consummation, *'they will look on the one they have pierced, and they will mourn for him as one mourns for an only child'* (Zechariah 12:10). The fulfilment of this prophecy is still missing: The acceptance of Yeshua as the Jewish Messiah by Israel.

Despite all these accomplishments, it became the conviction of a growing number: If God is fulfilling all the other prophecies; we must pay attention to the fulfilment of the other prophecy as well. Since 1967, more and more Jews from secular, conservative and even orthodox backgrounds are asking the question: What does this development mean in the light of Zechariah's prophecy. Could it be that the **'whom'** might be the one the Jews on the streets call 'Yeshua' (for 'Jesus') – with an unquestionable negative connotation? Could it be that he is the true Messiah of Israel?

In the atmosphere after the Six Day War thousands and thousands of Jews, mostly university students, turned to Jesus.

This was especially true in the US where the movement was already establishing its own congregations. The pace in Israel was slower, but it did happen there too. It also occurred in European countries, such as England and France. In the former Soviet Union, after the Iron Curtain fell, thousands of Jews also put their faith in Yeshua. Thus, the years after 1967 were ones of great growth for Messianic Judaism.

FIVE

MESSIANIC JEWS IN THE WORLD TODAY

TODAY, THE MESSIANIC JEWISH MOVEMENT is well established – relatively small, but strong. There are around 100,000 Messianic Jews worldwide. In their congregations maybe another 200,000 partly Jewish or Gentile relatives and friends have found their home. Their influence on both Jewish and Christian societies is much stronger than one might imagine. The faith of these Messianic Jews is expressed with deep conviction, with dedication and passion for the Lord.

There are Messianic congregations practically everywhere where there is some concentration of Jews. It is estimated that there are approximately 15,000 to 16,000 Messianic Jews living their witness in Israel, gathering in almost 130 congregations. Depending on how one describes a congregation, there are 350–400 congregations in the United States. About the same number exists in Russia, (This is because this movement grew rapidly after the end of the Soviet Union). There are also up to 5,000 believers gathering in Messianic Jewish congregations in Germany, mostly Russian-speaking, immigrants from the former Soviet Union countries.

The largest congregation of Messianic Jews in the world is currently located in Kiev, Ukraine, with over 2,000 members, 50% of them being Jewish. There are many smaller congregations belonging to this largest Messianic Jewish network in Ukraine, Moldavia, Belarus and Russia. Nowhere else in Europe is such a high number of Messianic congregations and House Churches found. There are Messianic groups in South Africa and other places in Africa and Asia. The numbers of all these are increasing rapidly within a relatively short period of time.

Just recently the world has become more aware of the tribes in Africa and Asia who claim to be descendants of the ten lost tribes of Israel (or descendants from the first diaspora). Many of these tribes have a 'Christian' history. They are now seeking a way to combine their claim of Hebrew ancestry with their more recent faith in Christ. Inevitably, new Messianic congregations will be formed.

All this Messianic witness is lived out often at a high price. Many Jewish circles consider the Messianic Jews a threat. The most radical expression of this enmity is found in the activities of some ultra-orthodox rabbinic groups in Israel and elsewhere who fear the influence of Messianic Jews so much that they are even willing to organise 'religious police troops.' An example would be the 'Yad L'achim' movement that often terrorises Messianic centres in Israel. To hinder Messianic Jews from bringing the Good News to their fellow Jews, they mobilise mass protests in the streets against the Messianic witness. Often, they even use acts of violence and physical aggression, such as beatings and bombs. All of this is a result of fear, a militant over-reaction to a group of faith-motivated Jews who desire to proclaim their beliefs in freedom.

MESSIANIC POTENTIAL IN ETHIOPIA

There are a number of congregations in Ethiopia. This is not surprising, as we know that Ethiopia was the only country in the world that had already developed in ancient times, an ongoing friendship and connection with the people of Israel. According to extra-Biblical traditions, King Solomon, the son of David, had an affair with the Queen of Sheba from Ethiopia, and a boy named Menelik was born as a result. Since then right up until the 1960s, this Kingly Jewish family ruled over Ethiopia until King Haile Selassie was murdered during a communist revolution. Even today, when someone visits the palace of the president (formerly 'The Kings Palace') you can find Jewish symbols everywhere, including the Star of David at the four corners of the presidential desk.

Not only has this royal family traced its heritage back to Jewish roots; even though the whole nation, its traditions and religious practices are part of the heritage of the Coptic Church, they have all been deeply influenced by Jewish customs and the Torah. The Coptic Church of Ethiopia imitates various Jewish rites: Women need to follow the Jewish health laws; people normally do not eat pork; laws according to the Torah regulate the processes of inheritance; the Coptic Church buildings are constructed according to a model similar to the Jewish Temple in Jerusalem, with a Holy of Holies in the centre. All this provides a very favourable environment for the growth of the Messianic Movement in the region.

Marrano History in South America and the Potential for the Movement

Of all continents, the Messianic Movement in South America has the greatest potential for growth. A high percentage of inhabitants of Spanish and Portuguese-speaking countries in Latin America are descendants of those Jews who fled to the colonies in the 16th century from the terror of the 'Catholic monarchs' and the Holy Inquisition that occurred on the Iberian Peninsula.

In the late 15th century, the so-called 'Catholic monarchs' of Spain, Queen Isabella of Aragon and King Fernando of Castile, and a little later, the Portuguese King Manuel (who married their daughter), wanted to take advantage of the Jews who lived in their kingdom. In Spain, they borrowed a lot of Jewish money to finance their wars against the Moors. Instead of paying back their debt, they decided in 1492 to pressure their Jewish creditors to become Christians, forcing them to be baptised. If they refused, the Jewish merchants stood to lose not only the return of their money but everything they had because they would then be expelled from the land.

The consequences of this decree of the monarchs was horrific. 600,000 Jews were living on the Peninsula at that time and according to most scholars, about 200,000 left the country instead of giving up their Jewishness. In the end, up to 400,000 agreed to be baptised. Those Jews who escaped from Spain to Portugal in the hope of freedom were, very shortly after, again forced to be baptised by King Manuel. King Manuel did not even offer the possibility of leaving the land to them, for he did not want to lose his best craftsmen and merchants. So, in the end, almost all Jews living on the Peninsula were baptised. But this did not bring freedom to them. The newly baptised, so-called 'Conversos' or New Christians and their Catholic life were carefully monitored for the next twenty years after their baptism. This 'monitoring' was done by the *'Holy Inquisition'*.

THE HORROR OF THE INQUISITION

This terrible system of Church control was invented and already perfected in the 14th century by Catholic religious orders like the Dominicans and Franciscans. It was used to terrorise these newly baptised Jewish families to make sure that the Conversos would not live a double life: Catholic Christians in public but, inside the privacy of their homes, still practicing Jews. These newly baptised Jews were often called 'Marranos', a Spanish word for 'pigs', because they had to eat pork publicly to prove that they had given up their entire Jewish heritage. The Holy Inquisition used every method imaginable to harass and persecute the Marranos. 'Old' Christians were forced to accuse their newly baptised Jewish neighbours of anything that might indicate some ongoing Jewish practice in their private homes. This produced for the Marranos a state of terror, living constantly under suspicion. To escape this pressure, finally many fled on ships to the colonies in South America. Throughout the 16th century these Conversos flooded countries like Brazil, Venezuela, Argentina, Chile and Mexico. But even there, they were not free. *The Inquisition* came right behind them and installed the same system of terror even in the New World.

There is an estimate that nowadays 20 to 25 million people in South America have Jewish blood as the descendants of these Marranos. Many of these families have decided to forget about it, abandoning any connection with Judaism and accepting the fact that they became Catholic or even turned away from any deep faith. But there are also families who held on to their Jewish identity over all those centuries, who managed to stay loyal to their people. In the secrecy of their homes, they continued keeping Jewish traditions, celebrating Shabbat, circumcising their boys, and even somehow observing the kashrut – the Jewish food laws. Nothing was done which would indicate their Jewishness outside the privacy of their own homes. Even as late as the 19th century, boys who attended Catholic private schools were still checked to verify whether or not they were circumcised. Even though they tried to hide it, it was quite easy to find out if families belonged to the Marranos or not. This situation of constant hiding was transmitted from generation to generation. Because of this double life, many of those Marrano families today have lost their sense of identity – they just do not know who they really are.

Over the centuries, millions of these Marranos didn't have the joy of being able to say: *'Jesus is a Jew, and so am I.'* But now, with the resurrected Messianic Jewish witness, it opens the door for them to express both sides of their identity fully – to be a full Jew and a full believer in Jesus at the same time. These Marrano families are a huge potential for growth of the Messianic Jewish Movement!

The history of *The Inquisition* in Europe and in South America is a bloody history. It was one of the cruellest sins committed by the Catholic Church in its history. I am convinced that until the Catholic Church, with a majority of its leaders, officially recognises this horrible sin against the Marrano Jews, many of the strong spiritual stumbling blocks that the Catholic Church faces in those parts of the world will not be lifted. This is particularly true for Spain, Portugal and South America. A powerful spiritual revival with all the fruit that it would bring cannot take place as long as this repentance is not forthcoming.

Concerning the Marrano Jews, it seems to me that the Holy Spirit is saying to the Catholic Church: *'Let my people go.'* The leadership of the Catholic Church, in recognition of its past guilt should demonstrate goodwill to repair the damage. They need to release these Marrano families to choose freely whether they want to continue to be Catholics or to live as Jews. Surely many will decide to become part of a Messianic Jewish movement. This would allow them to embrace their Jewishness and their faith in Jesus at the same time.

WHAT CHARACTERISES MESSIANIC JEWS TODAY?

Christology – They really do believe in Jesus according to the Apostolic Creed, just like the Gentiles. They not only believe in Him as Israel's Messiah, but also as the Saviour of the world and the Son of God. In some parts of the movement there is still a struggle with monophysitic tendencies in Christology, mostly over-estimating the human nature of Christ. Those congregations are mostly excluded from the main stream.

Trinity – Messianic Jews also believe in the Trinity, though they probably would not define their faith in the triune God by using the Greek theological language of the Nicene Creed. After all, the very term 'Trinity' is not found in the Scriptures. A Messianic Jewish way of understanding the deity usually follows a more Hebraic theological tradition but in the end the substance of believing in the unity of HaShem HaAv, HaBen VeHaRuach HaKodesh is the same as ours.

Baptism and The Lord's Supper – Messianic Jews are baptised as adults. No Messianic congregation that considers itself part of the mainstream would refuse to emphasise the central role of baptism in the name of Yeshua or the Trinity and with complete immersion into 'living' water. Most Messianic congregations celebrate some form of the Lord's Supper. There are many different models: the regular and liturgical form of celebration; the celebration that takes place regularly but more seldom; celebrations of the Lord's Supper only once a year at Pesach (Passover) - included in a Messianic Passover Haggadah (a Jewish text that sets forth the order of the Passover Seder or ritual); a more sacramental understanding of the Eucharist following High Church traditions; and an understanding of the Lord's Supper as a remembrance more or less following the reformed Church traditions. In general, many Messianic congregations are moving towards expressing themselves through a more Jewish form of liturgy.

Leadership - Messianic Jews ordain elders and deacons to govern their congregations, to pastor the flock and to officiate at their celebrations. There are a few congregational networks where elders are educated according to certain theological and pastoral curricula, and where the elders work closer together (i.e. UMJC, MJAA, Tikkun Network). The more autonomous congregations – completely independent in all their development and decision-making – are still the dominant reality in the movement. Some circles have started a discussion about apostolic leadership structures and how to link them to the apostolic authority of the first generation of Jewish believers. This discussion includes how to relate Messianic Jewish leadership to the apostolic succession highly valued in some historic Church streams.

The role of Biblical Scriptures – Contrary to the vast majority of rabbinical orthodoxy, Messianic Jews consider all parts of the Holy Scriptures central to all theology and doctrine. A clear priority is given to the Tanakh, (the Old Testament of which the Torah – the first five books of the Bible – is the most central part), reflected in the light of the New Testament scriptures. The Bible is clearly of higher authority than the Talmud and other sources of Jewish writings, which is a big difference between Messianic and Rabbinic Judaism. For some parts of the movement, Talmudic tradition is completely irrelevant. For others, it is an important vehicle to connect with traditional Judaism. Messianic Jews read the Bible with Jewish eyes and have established, over the last few decades, different schools of Hebraic hermeneutics.

Real Jews – However, Messianic Jews continue to be Jews. To be considered a Jew and be accepted among Jews, it is necessary to follow the fundamental practices of Judaism.

The more they live a truly Jewish life, the more they are respected as part of the Jewish people.

- **Circumcision** – For the mainstream of the Messianic Jews, it is a 'must' to keep this sign of the covenant as the spiritual connection with the Jewish people.
- **Shabbat** – Celebrated in most congregations, instead of Sunday as the Lord's Day, it starts on Friday evening with the Erev Shabbat (a family celebration) and ends at sundown on Saturday evening. Even though Messianic Jews follow the traditional Jewish form for Shabbat with their prayers and songs, they place Yeshua into the centre of Shabbat.
- **Kashrut** – Adhering to the most central of kosher requirements, many Messianic Jews call this 'Biblically kosher,' which can mean abstaining at least from pork, unclean sea food and other unclean foods. Only a few families separate meat and milk in the kitchen following traditional kashrut.
- **Family rituals** – Bat and bar mitzvah, weddings, and burial ceremonies are all celebrated within the Messianic Community according to Jewish traditions. Because the Messianic Movement is still relatively young, often there is no Messianic rabbi available to officiate over these ceremonies. In some cases, such as the brit milah (circumcision on the 8th day after birth), the Messianics need to find an orthodox rabbi to assist them.
- **Jewish feasts and holidays** – These are celebrated by most congregations. This is at least true for the high feasts:

- Pesach and The Feast of Unleavened Bread;
- The Feast of First Fruits – the Shabbat after Pesach;
- Shavuot (Pentecost) – 49 days or seven weeks after (also known as the celebration of the giving of Torah);
- Rosh Hashanah – the Feast of the Shofars, the Jewish New Year;
- Yom Kippur – the Day of Atonement, the holiest day for the Jews;
- Sukkot - (Feast of Tabernacles)

The Jewish feasts and holidays are, perhaps, the strongest connection to the Jewish people. They teach the next generation the Jewish history of salvation and how to understand and keep their heritage. At the same time, they interpret the prayers and traditions according to their meaning in the light of the Messiah – His redeeming work and His Second Coming.

Law and Redemption – For Messianic Jews, the living under the Law and following Jewish traditions is not required in order to be accepted by God or even saved. In the mainstream of the movement, the question of redemption is clearly kept separate from obedience to Jewish heritage. It is the blood of the Lamb of God, which rectifies and saves by Grace alone. Living in obedience to Torah and keeping the Jewish lifestyle is a question of identification with the Jewish people and its ongoing priestly ministry among the nations of the earth. Many Messianic Jews understand Torah as 'a set of Instructions, from a father to his children' to foster obedience and train them. *'Listen, my son, to your father's instruction and do not* *forsake your mother's teaching [Torah]'* (Proverbs 1:8). It's the way to introduce the next generation into their style of living.

There are extreme attitudes regarding the place of Torah at both ends of the movement. There are those who call themselves Messianic Jews but refuse, with conviction, any form of classic rabbinic obedience to Torah. There is the other extreme – those in the movement who make the keeping of the Law the decisive turning point not only for being a Messianic Jew but even for being a true Gentile disciple of Yeshua. This way some even require Torah observance from those Gentile believers who want to be in good standing with the living God and in communion with the Messianic Jewish part of the Church. They are interpreting the Gospel of Jesus in a rather extreme form and by that, develop an almost sectarian form of Messianic Judaism. All these extremes confuse and weaken the movement.

For the Messianic Jew, living out Torah means taking part in the priestly vocation of all of Israel. While the relationship with God is only defined by faith in the Messiah and His redemption, obedience to Torah expresses this identification with the Jewish people and its eschatological ministry. Because of this, the Torah is not taken word for word but has to be interpreted under the guidance of the Holy Spirit. The isolated 'letter' kills. The Law of God is written onto our hearts by the Spirit of God, according to the prophecy of Ezekiel (36:26-27). Following this spirit-filled interpretation of Torah brings life and will bring all of society into the Kingdom of Heaven.

NOT EVERYONE CALLING HIMSELF A MESSIANIC JEW – IS INDEED ONE

Wearing a tallit, a yarmulke (kippah) or singing Jewish songs does not make someone Jewish. To be a Jew, someone must fit into one of these two requirements: having Jewish blood, or joining the Jewish people as a proselyte, which includes being willing to live a full Jewish life. If you have Gentile blood and claim to be a Messianic Jew, you must be willing to be circumcised and live under Jewish Law.

Most Messianic Jewish theologians would agree that a group can only be called a Messianic congregation when a significant percentage (at least one third) of the members have Jewish blood. There are various Messianic groups in which even the pastor is a Gentile. This is not acceptable for most Messianic theologians, because the Jewish people at large would never take such a congregation seriously as part of their people. Also, the Historic Churches look at such congregations as simply another expression of Evangelicalism.

An Evangelical congregation should not be called a Messianic congregation just because the group celebrates with some Jewish symbols and practices. Gentile Christian congregations that do so can cause harm. It is problematic when Gentile believers copy aspects of Judaism. Judaising the Church is neither the right way to restore the Jewish roots of the Church nor to prepare for the end times. Gentiles should continue to be authentic believers and Messianic Jews should maintain their identity as Jews. Together, we are united by our faith in the same Lord and Saviour. If we agree that it is God's intention to use the Messianic Jews to bring the Jewish people to their Messiah, then they need to maintain their clear identity as Jews and, at the same time, be firmly built on pure faith in the grace of Jesus.

Messianic Jews and Torah

One of the central debates within Messianic Judaism is still the question of how to relate to Torah. The five books of Moses are the key focus in Judaism. Every devout Jew has the desire to identify with and claim for himself the heritage of these books. The more they observe Torah, the more they are fulfilling their calling as Jews. For the Orthodox Jew, it means to be close to God.

But what does it then mean that Yeshua already fulfilled all the requirements of Torah in His life and death, and made us free from legalistic interpretations, human effort and obligations? There is much diversity within the Messianic Movement about this central question. Basically, there are five different groups, ranging from a more legalistic and literal understanding to a more spiritual and liberal approach: Neo-Ebionites, the Neo-Nazarenes (better known as 'Post Missionary Messianic Judaism'), the Messianic Jewish Orthodox, Evangelical Messianic Judaism and 'Jesus-Only Jews'. The middle three groups on the list represent the mainstream of the Messianic Movement while the first and last group represents the extremes.

> **The Neo-Ebionites** – According to this group, every Jew must keep the full Law. Often from their perspective,

keeping the Law can be more important than a relationship with Jesus or His place as the Son of God and Saviour. Their Christology is often not clear in comparison to the Apostolic Creed. Even the Gentile believers are required to live according to the complete Law. Gentile believers who are not willing to live the Torah lack the full redemption and cannot stay in full relationship with Messianic Jews. This extreme position does not represent the mainstream of the Movement.

The Neo-Nazarenes – This group is close in their identity and practice to what we know from the New Testament about the group of Jewish believers around James, the brother of Jesus. Among Neo-Nazarenes there is a tendency to emphasise sometimes even over-emphasise the Law. They are very attached to rabbinic Judaism. Many of them keep strictly to the precepts and traditions of Jewish life. They do this in the conviction that the Messianic Movement needs the rabbinic heritage as the only possible connection to the first century Messianic Jewish generation. Rabbinic Judaism helps them to cultivate an authentic Jewish heritage in their midst. However, while they may focus on Talmudic traditions, at the same time they never leave any room for doubt that salvation comes only by grace through the atonement of Jesus on the cross. This stream is often called 'Post-Missionary-Messianic-Judaism'. Supporters of this group are convinced that, indirectly, every Jew is connected to the redeeming work of the Jewish Messiah, some, even before their conversion. This fact raises in their understanding, questions about any type of 'life or death-evangelism'.

Messianic Jewish Orthodoxy – strongly emphasises the Abrahamic covenant rather than the one on Sinai. These people emphasise the gift of grace and the new freedom found in the Messiah. This conviction is combined with the inner obligation to keep the Law in obedience to Israel's election. The Law is lived out in their circles with a certain freedom from the rabbinic interpretation. They believe it is important to do as Jesus did: He fulfilled the Torah apart from the boundaries of Rabbinic interpretation. His word and His life as the 'new Moses' are the authentic interpretation. Many representatives of this party link their practice to the Apostle Peter and his careful walk between obedience and freedom.

Evangelical Messianic Judaism – This form of Messianic Judaism is probably the largest group in Israel. The message of redemption in the Messiah by grace alone is dominant in all that they preach and do. The role of the Law is viewed in a way similar to how the Apostle Paul saw it: For Jews, they are to live like faithful Jews; for Gentiles, they are to live a moral life but are free from the Law (Acts 15). This means that they might even eat pork on the rare occasions where this would be a sign of politeness to their Gentile hosts in times of travel. For the sake of loyalty to the Jewish people, they see it as right for them to keep the traditions as much as possible. They express their Jewishness in a minimum of at least four points: Keeping Shabbat and the Feasts, valuing Jewish heritage, circumcising the boys, and eating 'Biblically kosher' food or at least abstaining from unclean meats. They do this to be identified with the traditional Jewish community, and to thereby keep their access to the Jews. At the same time, they do not consider rabbinic tradition as a point of reference and orientation. Instead they criticize any dependency by Messianic Jews on orthodox Jewish legalistic practice.

Jesus-Only Jews – They stand for a particular form of Messianic Judaism, which emphasises the statement: 'Jesus - my everything'. Being his disciple is almost seen as a substitute for being Jewish. Therefore, they do not value the particular Jewish laws within Torah. They stress the principle of Paul: *'There is neither Jew nor Gentile, neither slave nor free, nor is there male and female, for you are all one in Christ Jesus.'* (Gal 3: 28). In a certain way they believe that the time of the Torah is over. Not only Gentiles are completely free from any particular Jewish Torah observation, but so are the Messianic Jews. The more they assimilate into Christian ways of expression, the better they fulfill the dramatic change from Law to Grace. Still many among them keep some nostalgic signs of identification, such as wearing a necklace with the Star of David or singing Jewish songs. But whatever they still do that is 'Jewish', they do not do it as an act of obedience, but rather to keep relationships intact with their Jewish relatives. They feel so completely free from Jewish tradition that many even cease to circumcise their children. This way of handling Jewishness is quite problematic for the other parts of the movement.

SIX

A CATHOLIC DIALOGUE WITH THE MESSIANIC JEWS

A TERRIBLE HISTORY OF THE CATHOLIC CHURCH'S DEALING WITH THE JEWS.

THE HISTORY OF THE CATHOLIC CHURCH with the Jews has been tragic over a long period of time. They were treated as second class citizens. They became isolated into Ghettos (e.g. Rome – since 1555). They were forced into conversion and baptism. The baptised Jews were treated like prisoners under the controlling system of the so called 'Holy Inquisition'. One text out of the catechism of 'The Society of Pope Pius X' (issued in 1997), an ultra-Catholic group at the fringe of the Church demonstrates the problematic position of traditional Catholicism for centuries. *'The Jews reject – as do all of those false religions – the Saviour, Jesus Christ. If Judaism was the true religion before the coming of Christ, it is no longer so now, because it did not recognise its hour and has not accepted its Redeemer. The true Jews have turned to Christ, with whose arrival the Jewish religion of the first covenant has lost its meaning and its right to exist'.*

There were always protesting voices from single members of the Church - but these were always drowned out. Nevertheless these 'prophetic' voices before the Vatican Council had already challenged the Church to change its perspective (e.g. Jacques Maritain with his paper 'Le Mystère d'Israel – Israel's mystery' or Hans-Urs von Balthasar with his paper 'Lonesome dialogue'). Lately when Catholic theologians and Church-leaders were confronted with the Nazi Holocaust – a dramatic reconsidering began. The great breakthrough happened with the Second Vatican Council and the document on the Jews 'Nostra Aetate' – issued in 1965.

THE ROLE OF POPE JOHN XXIII
TO BRING A BREAKTHROUGH

Pope John XXIII played a significant part in this fundamental change during Vatican II. Archbishop Angelo Giuseppe Roncalli (1881-1963) had always been a great friend of the Jews. As Papal Apostolic Delegate for Turkey and Greece (1935-1944) he organised a refuge for many Jews to flee to Palestine via Turkey and by that he saved about 24,000 Jews. Already, shortly after he had become Pope John XXIII he pressed on to issue a pro-Jewish-declaration to improve their relationship with the Catholic Church. He wanted to change all anti-Jewish teaching in the Church and to make it clear that the diaspora of the Jews is not a punishment from God for the crucifixion of Jesus.

When the idea of a new Council was launched by Pope John he made a significant assignment: the document on the Jews should be placed in the area of ecumenism, because the identity of the Church and the topic of Christian unity are highly related to the mystery of Israel. The first draft for such a Council Decree (*'Decretum de Iudaeis'* 1961) was stopped because of the strong opposition of Arabic bishops fearing the political pressure on the Christians living in Arabic countries, if such a decree was issued (see: 'Wardi-affair'). Nevertheless,

Pope John pressed on. It was his last intervention as Pope, just a few days before his death, to let everyone know that this project had to be finished. The declaration *'Nostra Aetate'* *('In our Time')* was finally passed on October 28th in 1963, after many long and difficult debates. It was often called *'the shortest, but most significant document of the Council'* (Cardinal Franz König), a document trying to overcome a horrible history of over 1800 years in only 500 words!

Only the 4th chapter dealt with the Jewish people. Herein the Church declares, that she is *'spiritually connected'* with Israel through the common progenitor Abraham. The Patriarchs, Moses and the Prophets are mentioned as common heritage - belonging to the *'Church before the Church'*. The Church acknowledges that she has received the revelation of the Old Testament through the covenant of the people of Israel. The document emphasises the significance of the Jews for salvation history not only in the past but also in the future, because *'(The Church has)... been grafted in among the others and now share in the nourishing sap from the olive root.'* (Rom 11:17) At least indirectly Nostra Aetate says: *whoever declares Israel of no significance for salvation history denies himself the possibility of being grafted in as a wild shoot and deprives himself of the strength coming from the root.*

In defending the canonicity of the Old Testament (which was questioned by the anti-Jewish paradigm of Marcion the heretic in the 2nd century) the documents make clear that *'In the Church's opposition to him she defended Israel's legacy and its lasting importance for the Church.'* God is the author of both Testaments, which results in the fact that Israel and the Church are connected by a common bond. Even though the vast majority of the Jews did not recognise Jesus as Messiah, Israel remains in the irrevocable covenant, her gifts and calling are *'without regret'* (Rom 11:28 f).

Nostra Aetate finally rejects the concept of a Jewish collective guilt for Jesus' death on the cross. The Council also *'regrets hatred, persecution and manifestations of anti-Semitism'*. Jews are *'neither to be described as rejected nor cursed by God'*, because such a description contradicts the Holy Bible. As a consequence, the Church´s teaching has to be cleansed from all anti-Judaism. Even though the document doesn´t speak against mission in general, it judges a certain form of evangelistic arrogance.

Unfortunately, Nostra Aetate does not touch the subject of eschatology. It could have said that the Jewish end time expectation of the Messiah and the Christian hope for His Parousia lead to a convergence of hope! Many theologians criticize the fact that in 'Lumen Gentium' (Nr.16), the main document of the Council, the relationship with the Jews is described after the model of gradual affiliation to the Church, which does not sufficiently value the fact that Israel is not on the fringe of the Church but rather belongs to its innermost self-image. Another issue which was untouched is the land question. In Nostra Aetate the Catholic Church was not able to make even one positive statement about the independent Jewish State, even though she knew how much the land of the promise is part of Israel's identity. And it took the Vatican until 1993 to come to the *'Fundamental Agreement between the Holy*

See and the State of Israel'. The pressure against such a treaty from the Arab (Christian) side was overwhelming. This is why many Jewish comments after the promulgation of Nostra Aetate: said critically: *'With that (statement), is not the outstretched hand being pulled back halfway?'*

THE WORK OF POST-NOSTRA AETATE POPES

In a creative continuation after Nostra Aetate, the post-Conciliar Popes: Paul VI, John Paul II and Benedict XVI have accepted the legacy of Nostra Aetate as a holy commission. Paul VI (1962 – 1978) was the first Pope in history to go on a pilgrimage to the Holy Land in 1964. In acknowledgement of the foundational role of the Jews both for the Church and for Christian unity, he also assigned the *'Commission for Religious Relations to Judaism'* institutionally into the Pontifical Council for Promoting Christian Unity.

In 1974 the **Vatican Commission for Religious Relations with the Jews** issued a document: '…The problem of Jewish-Christian relations concerns the Church as such…Pondering her own mystery…she encounters the mystery of Israel. Therefore, even in areas where no Jewish communities exist, this remains important…The very return of Christians to the sources and origins of their faith, grafted onto the earlier covenant, helps the search for unity in Christ, the cornerstone.' (Cardinal Willebrands). This document indirectly indicates that a healed relationship between the Church and the Jews will help the Church to heal its own internal divisions, between the denominations.

John Paul II (1978-2005). Growing up as a Polish boy close to Auschwitz, he always had strong personal relationships with Jews. During his first visit as a Pope to Auschwitz-Birkenau in 1979, he called the Concentration Camp of Auschwitz 'the Golgotha of our times' to express the deep connection between the suffering of the Jewish people and the suffering of its Jewish Messiah. In 1980, during his encounter with the 'Central Council of Jews' in Germany, he spoke about 'the encounter between...the people of the Old Covenant, which has never been revoked, and the people of the New Covenant'. On another occasion he said: '...*the encounter between Catholics and Jews is not an encounter of two ancient religions, which are each going their own way. Rather there is a proximity, which is based on the mystical bond*' a bond that '*in Abraham brings us close together and through Abraham to God, who has elected Israel and made the Church emerge out of Israel*'.

Unfortunately, this word triggered **the theory of a dual way to salvation.** This question has some value: how is the eternal validity of God's covenant with Israel to be reconciled with the conviction of the newness of the New Covenant that Jesus has brought? Unfortunately, theologians on both sides answered this question with the theory of two parallel ways to salvation – or as it often is called – the 'Two Covenant Theology' (e.g. the writings of Friedrich-Wilhelm Marquardt and Paul Van Buren: A Christian Theology of the People of Israel, New York, 1983). This most problematic theory simply says: there is one way to salvation for the Jews - through their faith and life under Torah and there is another way for the nations - through their faith in Christ. That would mean that Israel is going to be saved without needing Jesus Christ. This position contradicts the fact that the Messiah *from* Israel is also the Messiah *for* Israel, forgetting that the Gospel quotes Jesus saying: *'I was sent only to the lost sheep of the House of Israel...'*.

In 1985 the '**Notes on the Correct Way to Present Jews and Judaism in Preaching and Catechesis in the Roman Catholic Church**' (No. I.7) – published by the Vatican – explicitly rejected this perspective: *'Jesus affirms that there shall be 'one flock and one shepherd' (Jn 10:16). The Church and Judaism cannot then be seen as parallel ways of salvation and the Church must witness to Christ as the Redeemer for all 'while maintaining the strictest respect for religious liberty in line with the teaching of the Second Vatican Council declaration 'Dignitatis Humanae'*.

In 1999 the Vatican document **Dominus Jesus** rebukes even more strongly any attempt to diminish the redemptive role of Christ for any human society – including the Jews. Although there is the unrevoked covenant of God with Israel, the need for the universal role of Jesus Christ as redeemer includes all Jewish men and women. This 'salvational universalism' provides the hope that all of Israel at the end of days will accept the Christ of the Parousia as their Messiah and will be saved through him.

During a visit of John Paul II - as the first Pope ever to visit the Great Synagogue in Rome in 1986 – he made an act of repentance for the enforcement of Christian beliefs onto the Jews of the Ghetto in earlier centuries. After that the Pope emphasised: *'The Jewish religion is not something external but belongs in a certain way to the centre of our religion. You are our favoured brothers and, one could even say, our older brothers'.* With that word the constitutive importance of Judaism for the Christian Church was unshakably affirmed. In a similar way in 1988 John Paul II stated before a group of Jewish leaders that *'...According to the teaching of the Second Vatican Council, she* (the Church) *should better understand her bond with you* (the Jews)... *by meditating upon her own mystery. Now that mystery is rooted in the mystery of the person of Jesus Christ, a Jew, crucified and glorified'* (John Paul II; Spiritual Pilgrimage; 126f.) All of this has been worked out in more detail in the course of the official Jewish/Catholic Dialogue.

The **Vatican Commission for Religious Relations with the Jews,** in 2011– with a strong connection to Pope Benedict XVI – published a new series of studies under the title: *'Christ Jesus and the Jewish People Today: New Exploration of Theological Interrelationships'*. The outcome is a Torah Christology which leads to an Israel-Christology opening the path towards an Israel-Ecclesiology.

Torah Christology & Israel-Ecclesiology

The identity of the Church is rooted in Christ. The identity of Christ is rooted in his relationship with the Jewish people. Therefore, the identity of the Church is inseparable from Israel. The important question still is: how are they related? If the Jewish people and their faith are 'intrinsic' to the very identity of the Church, then the Church´s theological vision of herself (her ecclesiology) must reflect this truth. This view raises questions for many aspects of Catholic theology, from

Christology to Eschatology, from liturgy to the sacraments (*see Cardinal Willebrands; Church and Jewish People, 28*).

In a certain way by living under the Torah Israel fulfils its priestly vocation. As Jesus is the fulfilment of the Torah in His person, He is also the embodiment of all that Israel should have and should be. Cardinal Aron Jean Marie Lustiger (1929-2007), a Jew and a Holocaust survivor, made Catholic Archbishop of Paris stated this truth, even more clearly, in his major work on his Jewish identity (The Promise; 33-39). For him the incarnation of the Torah in Jesus is not just a spiritual truth, it is the fruit of His being integrated into the real life of the Jews around Him and by their being integrated into the history of His Jewish people, to whom He was given by the Father as the eternal Son.

Out of this very concrete incarnation in and through the flesh of Jewish Miriam of Nazareth, Jesus is the perfect representative and individual embodiment of the Jewish people. As the Son of Israel – He is The Son of the Father. As the King of Israel – He is the Messiah and Christ. The figure (sign) of Jesus is at the same time the figure (sign) for and of Israel and, by that the figure, for and of the Church. What is said of one can be applied to the other. Jesus can only be understood in this loyalty to His people who are first of all Israel and only secondarily the Church of the nations.

As the son of Israel, He is inseparably the Son of God. Even though He fulfils Israel´s commission in His life, death and resurrection, He is not the substitute for Israel, but rather the very realisation of Israel's vocation to be God's Son as a whole people. He fulfils the Law (as God intended) completely and perfectly, and so He acts as the true Israel should act. This total identification with Israel, as He embodies His people, does not only affect the Jews of His day but affects all members of Israel of both past and future generations. That means that all the sufferings of Israel (even those caused by the Church) are part of Christ's passion, are part of the mystery of the Cross. This includes the killing of the children of Bethlehem but also the Holocaust (Cardinal Lustiger; The Promise; 50).

For Christians this means – not as the cause of their salvation by the blood of Jesus but as a fruit of it – they should imitate Jesus as the embodiment of the Torah and follow him in discipleship, and therefore keep the Torah in a spiritual way. This brings Christians even without their knowing it into a life-giving relationship with the Jewish people.

For Jews it means that whenever they obey the Torah as Jews, they strive towards the goal of being an incarnation of the Torah, as Jesus is. This living according to the Torah does not bring redemption to Jews, which can only be received by the Grace of the atonement by the Lamb alone. But any Jew reaching out to live according to the Torah is already somehow orienting himself - maybe even without knowing it - towards the life-giving and salvific communion with Christ, in whom this incarnation of the Torah comes to its completion and fulfilment.

For both Jews and Christians this longing only comes to

completion and full fruition when this direct or indirect relationship with the Torah is realised in an active conversion and faith in Jesus the Messiah.

The realisation of this theological truth by no means takes place easily or automatically. *'The Church of The Circumcision'*, the Jewish part of the Church, is meant to be a mediator between the two groups, helping each of them to understand this mystery and to live according to Torah as the fruit of a salvific relationship with Yeshua. It would be much easier for both sides to see and understand this mystery if there were to exist 'The Church of The Circumcision' as a bridge between the two. The Son of God, incarnated in the Jewish people, made two people one in His flesh on the Cross (Eph 2: 14-17). The Jewish part of the Church (ecclesia ex Judais) is the spiritual and natural bond between the Church from the nations and Rabbinic Judaism, as this Jewish part of the Church lives out the Sinai covenant in their explicit confession and discipleship to Yeshua, the risen Messiah, as the fulfilment of the Torah.

ENCOUNTER IN THE VATICAN

In 1998, a group of three Messianic Jewish leaders, Msgr. Peter Hocken, a priest from England, and I, a Catholic deacon from Austria went to meet with Cardinal Josef Ratzinger in the Vatican, at that time still the Prefect of the Congregation for Church Doctrine, later to become Pope Benedict XVI. When the Messianic representatives shared their personal testimonies of how they came to accept Jesus as their Messiah, the Cardinal listened carefully. After a long pause of thoughtful silence, he finally said: *'The Church will not be complete unless it exists out of both the Church out of the Jews and the Church out of the Gentiles (ecclesia ex Judais & ecclesia ex Gentibus.'* He continued with another important statement. *'We theologians always knew that one day you (referring to the Messianic brothers) would need to appear. None of us could imagine how this would happen.'* He mentioned that as he is listening to their witness, an important question had to be raised: Is this Messianic witness an authentic experience? If this phenomenon is proved authentic, does that mean that this Movement is an eschatological sign? All present in the room were astounded! Who could expect such words – especially when one considers who was speaking. In essence, what the Cardinal was indirectly saying was that even though the Holy Spirit throughout the centuries has preserved the Church, the Church today, because she lacks her Jewish component, is still incomplete.

For many centuries before the *Second Vatican Council* (1962-65), it was Catholic consensus that the Church as such is a perfect society. But then Josef Ratzinger, the chief theologian of the Church, was indirectly saying, to the three Messianic leaders: The Church is complete only when the Jewish part of the Church is restored. It seemed that in the understanding of the Cardinal this restoration would require that at least a part of Israel is recognising Jesus as their Messiah. So, consequently, the question for the Cardinal was: Is this movement the first fruit of Israel's recognition of her Messiah? Does this movement have the potential to begin the restoration of the Jewish part of the Church, which had been lost in the fourth century? Referring to the 'eschatological sign' means nothing less than that this movement indicates that the Second Coming of Jesus is close!

Another important figure in the Vatican had an eye-opening encounter with two prominent Israeli Messianic leaders: the theologian of the papal household, the later Cardinal George Cottier OP. Shortly after this meeting with Cottier it was followed by another meeting between them and Pope John Paul II. These meetings so inspired all of them, that the Pope, Cardinal Ratzinger and George Cottier decided to begin a non-public dialogue between Catholics and Messianic Jews, starting in the year 2000. Ten Messianic theologians and ten Catholic theologians began dialoguing with each other year by year for the next 14 years for almost a week each time, meeting alternatively in Rome and in Israel. Cardinal Cottier reported directly to the Pope about the positive developments within this dialogue-group.

The main goal of the dialogue was to clarify one question: Is this Messianic Jewish movement a serious phenomenon coming from the Holy Spirit, or is it fake – a kind of disguised evangelical church with Jewish elements? If it should turn out that this movement should be taken seriously, then there would be many consequences for the Catholic Church. I have myself been part of this dialogue right from the beginning. In 2015, after Cardinal Christoph Schönborn from Vienna, Austria, had finally taken over chairmanship from the aging Cardinal Cottier, a report was presented to Pope Frances by some of the members of this group summarising 14 years of hard theological investigation. The conclusion was: This Messianic phenomenon is real! Because of this positive result, the dialogue will continue now in an official form. The right place for this process of finding theological consensus has still to be found within the Vatican structures in order to bring about the greatest chance of the most practical results. What has become clear to some important leaders in the Vatican – although certainly not to all – could and should become clear to other leaders of the Christian Churches.

SEVEN

A CHALLENGE FOR THE GENTILE CHURCHES

THE MESSIANIC MOVEMENT IS NOT A FAKE. On the contrary, it's a challenge to the Christian world to reconsider its theological make-up. The Christian Churches are confronted with an unexpected partner. This means we need to think and to act quite differently in the future than we have in the past.

Understanding the Mystery of the Olive Tree – The principle Paul explains in Rom 11:16-24 with the image of the Olive Tree needs to be understood by all Gentile believers before we are motivated and able to do more for the Messianic Movement.

- We Gentile believers are the grafted in branches of the Olive Tree of Israel, grafted in by the blood of the Jewish Messiah.
- This blood has made us 'spiritually' pure and by that – without a biological bloodline – we have become members of the 'commonwealth of Israel'. Spiritually we are linked to the Jewish people without becoming Jews. It is told that Pope Pius XI. – confronted with the horror of NAZI-Antisemitism made the strong statement that 'we Christians are all Jews in the spiritual of the word'.
- We Gentiles only have a position in salvation history because we are a part of God's Chosen People.
- We are connected to Israel through the Jewish part of

the Church. This relationship with Israel is only able to be completely realised (not only as an indirect spiritual bond as expressed in the last part of chapter 6) when there is a Messianic Jewish movement to form a bridge between the Jewish people and the Gentile believers.

The Messianic Jewish Movement is an authentic phenomenon – The Catholics are not the only ones who researched this movement. Other churches began their investigations as well. In most cases, the outcome was the same: this is an authentic movement within Judaism! More and more theologians agree that this is, or could be, the beginning of the turning of the Jews to Jesus as their Messiah. Things that still prevent Christian leaders from acknowledging this movement are:

- different parts of the movement have different criteria as to what counts for someone to be considered a Jew;
- there is no common theology among the Messianic Community;
- there are no common standards of living and celebration;
- there is as yet no single, recognised authority to speak for the entire movement and, lastly;
- the movement continues to experience major frictions between various groups.

Yet, the general conclusion of the dialogue remains correct even though the movement is immature. Despite these negative facts, Christianity cannot ignore this phenomenon any longer. It is one of the most impressive signs of our time.

Overcoming and renouncing all forms of Replacement Theology in the churches – In the 4th chapter of the document about the relationship between the Catholic Church and the Jewish people under the title '**Nostra Aetate**' ('*In our Time*') the Catholic Church officially repudiated Replacement Theology. What a great step forward! Even though the document did hesitate to explain fully the role of the Jewish people in God's economy and avoided mentioning anything about the special role of Jews in the Catholic Church or about the Messianic Jews as such, it finally opened the door for a dialogue between the Catholics and the Jews and gave us the foundation for the dialogue between the Catholics and the Messianic Jews.

In December 2015, another document was issued by the Vatican entitled '**50 Years after Nostra Aetate**.' This new paper went further in repudiating Replacement Theology and announcing the need for the Church to be well grounded on the foundation of its Jewish roots. The new document also strongly opposed any form of 'Dual Covenant Theology,' a theological misunderstanding proclaiming that the Jews will be saved by their obedience to Torah while, at the same time, the Gentiles are saved through the atonement of Christ. Finally, the document speaks about avoiding any form of institutional mission to the Jews. Christians, in earlier centuries, have been responsible for imposing their Christian faith on the Jewish people. That should never happen again.

Unfortunately, what was still missing in the 2015 document was any reference to the phenomenon of Messianic Judaism or about the relationship between the Church and the

Messianic Jews. Probably such a statement was omitted to avoid the risk that support of the Messianic Jews by the Catholic Church could be interpreted as a new form of indirect, institutionally endorsed Christian mission towards the Jews.

All Christian denominations and independent churches need to repudiate Replacement Theology. Many of the historic Protestant churches have already done so. Interestingly, although many leaders of evangelical independent churches have experienced great revivals, many are still adherents of Replacement Theology, that is, preaching that the Church has replaced the old Israel (under the law) with the 'new Israel' (by the power of the Spirit). All historic, Charismatic, Pentecostal and Evangelical churches need to prepare official documents proclaiming in unison: *'We recognise our mistakes and sins of the past against the Jews. We want to forsake these offences. We want to recognise the freedom and identity of the Jews, because we can never replace them or take their unique place in the Church and in God's plan.'*

Of course, believing that official documents will solve the problem is an illusion. But, it would be a crucial beginning! Even though *Nostra Aetate*, and the document fifty years after, did change a great deal in the Catholic Church, more has to be changed in the thinking of Church members. Even today, many priests would not be able to articulate the Catholic Church's relationship with Israel. Documents are good, but they need to change people's hearts and minds. It is not enough for churches to produce papers. The message needs to be proclaimed and repeatedly taught in church services for as long as it takes to impact people effectively and change their way of thinking.

Recognition and Confession of all the sins against the Jewish people –The Church needs to recognise its sin against the Jews. This sin was not mere ignorance – this was the fruit of jealousy of the people of Israel, who are called in the Bible the '*Apple of His Eye'(Zech 2). This* sin is of such gravity; *it made the heart of God the Father suffer.* This sin of the Church cannot be viewed only through the eyes of historians since, in fact this sin is not a mere fact of history. This kind of sin has a very dangerous dynamic. If a sin like this is not dealt with, the results will last for generations and will bring death.

Again, an example out of my Catholic background: Pope John Paul II received very strong guidance of the Holy Spirit to apologise publicly to the Jews, in the name of the whole Church, for the sins committed against them in the past. For him, this was a necessary consequence resulting from the *Second Vatican Council* and the document '*Nostra Aetate.*' He wrote an encyclical letter to all the Catholic bishops inviting them into a time of humble reflection on the sins of the past, and to consider joining the pope in this act of 'cleansing of memory' over all these atrocities.

The first time that the Pope presented his idea to a group of cardinals, almost two years before the event took place; only a small minority of them gave positive feedback. Many cardinals strongly opposed the Pope and argued against his plans, reasoning that the 'Holy Church' never has to ask forgiveness because she cannot sin. They could not see that these horrible transgressions were collectively poisoning the Catholic Church over centuries. In their arguments, they contended that only individuals may be held accountable for their wrongdoing, for a sin they had directly committed. These cardinals denied that there was such a thing as culpability within the Church as such. This common sentiment was found among the Church Fathers, thereby motivating individuals in the hierarchy to inaugurate, or at least support, these atrocities against the Jewish people.

The Pope responded that, even though the Church is cleansed by the blood of Christ and made holy by Grace, the structural sins of a certain view, the wrong judgment of a whole system, had produced these horrible deeds of the Church as a society. These need to be confessed. Otherwise, this unconfessed structural sin remains a stumbling block against revival and restoration. This needs to be an act of humility by the Church as a whole because, as a community of believers, it has allowed this unbiblical teaching of replacement to blind the minds of its ministers and members.

The opposing cardinals could not prevent the Pope from following his conscience. On Ash Wednesday of the year 2000 in the Basilica of St. Peter he publicly asked forgiveness for the major sins of the Catholic Church in history – particularly for all the sins committed against the Jews. Here is the tragedy: Most Catholics and, indeed, nearly all of Christendom have never heard about this event.

Pope John Paul was guided by the Holy Spirit to repent twice. After he had done it in Rome, in the centre of the Catholic world, on behalf of all Catholics, the second act of humbling himself took place a few months later on in Jerusalem. He intended that it should be heard directly by all the Jews in the Land and in the Diaspora. As an old man, sick from Parkinson's disease, walking with great difficulty, he approached the Wailing Wall, putting a written note into one of the crevices between the huge stones of the Wall, which contained the same words of humble confession he had spoken in Rome. The whole Jewish world was deeply touched by his gesture – overwhelmed by the fact that such a courageous act had been taken by nobody less than the Pope himself - 1200 years after this persecution of the Jews by the Church began.

REPRESENTATIVE CONFESSION AND REPENTANCE

All Church leaders must do what the Pope did. However, we cannot wait until the very last superintendent, bishop or pastor wakes up. Those who are awake need to act now on behalf of those who sleep. The others will follow if some pioneers prepare the way. Even though Pope John Paul did something courageous – it is not enough. Christians in all denominations have to continue with this task of repentance, following the Pope's example of humility and repentance - until a significant change can be seen in those whose ancestors were once perpetrators and in those whose ancestors were once victims. This invitation for such a cleansing from the sins of the past has to be responded to by all who are ready now – prayer groups, prayer houses and spiritual communities. As we have not been the ones who committed the sins ourselves, we need to ask forgiveness in 'representative confession and repentance'. We have to do this on behalf of those in the past who died before they were able to understand their sin and repent publicly. These acts of confession are done not only on behalf of our ancestors, but also on behalf of the many today who are still unaware of this sinful past and its consequences and so are unwilling to undertake such an act of humility.

Daniel prayed to the living God that he and his ancestors have sinned against the Lord (Daniel 9:5-8). He, in his time, identified himself with the sins of his people. Representative prayer expresses: 'We and our fathers have sinned.' Identifying with the sins of past generations is a way to love, not to condemnation. Furthermore, it is a Biblical concept!

Representative confession means, first of all, identifying fully with those generations before us who sinned. From our ancestors, we have inherited the spiritual fruit of their sins. Such sin results in a certain spiritual blockage which cannot be removed by denial and continuing as if nothing had happened. There needs to be a deep identification with former generations and their sinful deeds and motives. We have to weep tears over 'our' sins. Why such an act of identification / repentance really works, bringing healing and freedom from the burden of the past and heavenly blessing that allows for a new start, remains a mystery.

Overcoming the sins against the Jewish part of the Church –
The Church not only needs to recognise its sin against the Jews

but also against the Jewish part of the Church – the sin of extinction of the *'ecclesia ex Judais'*. This was another consequence of the replacement lie. Before any reconciliation can happen between Jew and Gentile in the One Body of the Messiah there needs to be, first and foremost, a spiritual act of restoration, which includes identifying and confessing the sin. This is the only way to remove the spiritual blockages which prevent the restoration of the Jewish part of the Church. Without that, all our theological, diplomatic and promotional efforts for establishing Christian unity will be in vain.

There are still many Christian denominations which cannot see this sin of the past and are consequently opposing any welcome of the Messianic Jews into the Body of Messiah. This is particularly true for Christians from the Eastern Churches, which are more than reluctant to see the Messianic Jews as a missing component within the Church. For many Orthodox Christians the fact that some Jews have found their Messiah simply makes them wonder why they do not just integrate themselves into the structures of the Orthodox and Old Oriental Churches.

A lot of ignorance is still present. A persistent prayer movement among Catholics, Orthodox, Protestants, Evangelicals and Charismatics is needed to remove these obstacles. There is not yet enough openness among a majority of Christian leaders to receive the Jewish part of the Church back into their rightful place. We are far from this goal. An openness to welcome back the 'Older Brothers' will only be achieved through the eye-opening power of humility and intercession.

Only when we all feel the pain of the loss of the Jewish part of the Church, only when we all understand the high price the Church has had to pay and is still paying for the absence of our Jewish brethren, only then will we be able to weep and to repent.

A Spiritual battle – Satan has been working from the beginning of Salvation History to separate Israel from the nations, thereby dividing Jews and Gentiles in the one Church of the Messiah. As long as he prevents the effective union of these two groups, as long as the Gentile Church continues without its Jewish counterpart, Satan does not have to fear the victory of Christ on the cross. This is the great lie: that the Gentile Church can reach the ultimate goal of world redemption alone, without its Jewish brethren.

What blindness has covered the Church! To combat it, we need strong, united and persevering intercession. This blindness was the result of the arrogant and sinful way the Church dealt with God's chosen people. We have acted in a way that obstructed the divine plan of salvation, rather than cooperated with it. Thousands of intercessors need to devote their lives to prayer to overcome this lie. Because in this regard the majority of people in the Church are asleep, a group of pioneers will have to stand in the gap before the Lord on behalf of the blind.

The Church should see the Messianic Jews as an eschatological sign – Again, I am using an argument drawn from my Catholic background. In the Catechism of the Catholic Church (from 1983) we find the interesting paragraph, No. 674, *(see below)* which speaks about the time when all of Israel will turn their hearts to Yeshua as their Messiah. This will be the decisive criterion for releasing the Second Coming of the Lord. The coming of the glorious Messiah depends on 'all Israel' recognising Him. Before this catechism, the Catholic Church was very cautious when talking about the 'when and how' of the Second Coming. In its eschatological teaching, the Catholic Church usually emphasised individual eschatology – death, heaven, hell and purgatory. Since *Vatican Council II* , the Catholic Church has dramatically changed its relationship with the Jews. That opened the Church for a much clearer view of the central role of the Jewish people in salvation's history.

CCC No. 674
The glorious Messiah's coming is suspended at every moment of history until his recognition by 'all Israel', for 'a hardening has come upon part of Israel' in their 'unbelief' toward Jesus. St. Peter says to the Jews of Jerusalem after Pentecost: 'Repent therefore, and turn again, that your sins may be blotted out, that times of refreshing may come from the presence of the Lord, and that he may send the Christ appointed for you, Jesus, whom heaven must receive until the time for establishing all that God spoke by the mouth of his holy prophets from of old.' St. Paul echoes him: 'For if their rejection means the reconciliation of the world, what will their acceptance mean but life from the dead?' The 'full inclusion' of the Jews in the Messiah's salvation, in the wake of 'the full number of the Gentiles', will enable the People of God to achieve 'the measure of the stature of the fullness of Christ', in which 'God may be all in all.'

What does this theological statement say?

- Only the acceptance of Jesus as Messiah by a significant majority of the Jews will open the door for the Second Coming of the Lord. Heaven will hold Jesus back until the Jews begin to accept this truth. Our Christian *Hope* is totally dependent on what happens to the Jews in this regard.

- The catechism citing Romans 11:15: *'For if their rejection brought reconciliation to the world, what will their acceptance be but life from the dead?'* expects a massive worldwide evangelization after the Jews believe Jesus is, indeed, their Messiah.

- Only after Israel accepts Jesus as Messiah will all the Gentiles, now together with the Jewish believers, be able to come to the fullness of Christ. 'Fullness' means the completion and perfection of the Church. Wasn't this what Cardinal Ratzinger said – the Church is only complete when this happens?

The Messianic movement is an eschatological sign! The sudden growth of the Messianic movement is the beginning of the acceptance of Jesus by His own Jewish people. We must do everything within our power to see the movement increase and become mature. The unity of Jew and Gentile in the Church is, according to Paul and the Catholic Catechism, of significant importance for the 'if' and the 'how' of the Eschaton.

- **Relating to the Messianic Jewish movement in the right way** – We, as Gentile Christianity, cannot continue Church business as usual. God has resurrected the Messianic Community from the dead. They are given to us so that the Church will be complete again, as in the days of the Apostles. In order to see the ultimate fruit as soon as possible, we Gentiles must take action as a matter of urgency:

- **Welcome the Messianic Jews** – After we have annulled all the anti-Jewish decrees and every prohibition of the existence of a Jewish form of faith in Yeshua, the Messianic Jews need to experience our embrace and welcome. They are desperate, waiting for such an expression of love, especially from the historic Churches. This welcome must be real. This attitude would include: seeking them out in our cities, initiating contact, getting to know them personally and beginning relationships and friendships with them. And we need to do all of this even when we experience some Messianic Jews as fearful, keeping to themselves or even when they are cold and critical. The wounds of a long anti-Semitic history, which they share with all their non-messianic Jewish relatives, produced a prejudice toward all Gentile Christians, particularly against members of the historic churches, most of all the Catholic Church.

- **Friendship** – Reconciliation will only be affirmed in an atmosphere of real friendship. There is a need for growing fellowship between Messianic Jews and believers from the churches. Let us reconsider: How did the Jewish part of the Church die out in the 4th century? For the Gentile leaders of that day, it was no longer appropriate to have Messianic Jewish friends. Something parallel is going on today. Many Church leaders think it is shameful to be seen as a friend of Messianic Jews. They do not want to risk their good name among Orthodox Jews and highly academic theologians involved in Jewish Christian dialogue. This is not tolerable!!! We must offer our friendship, visiting their homes and their meetings, making our homes their homes, making clear that they are our brothers and sisters. Anything less will not be enough! If they cannot trust our friendship – they will isolate themselves again, feel rejected and hurt, and will form a closed and defensive movement. If this happens – it would be a great victory for Satan.

- **Recognition** – 'To honour' is the formal side of 'To welcome'. There is a need for a complete recognition of the movement in formal acts. Documents need to be issued – expressing the importance of the Messianic movement as part of the Body of Christ. These documents should strongly emphasise that we Christians see this movement as an integral part of Judaism, remaining authentically Jewish, while at the same time we consider them according to a 'bilateral ecclesiology' as being connected to the Christian Church. Other documents must clearly say to the Jewish world that the churches must not use this movement as an institutional form of Church mission to the Jews.

- **Loyalty** – However, a public proclamation of this nature will challenge the Christian-Jewish dialogue. The Church will need great wisdom to preserve their relationship with classic

Judaism while pursuing fellowship with the Messianic Community. The Messianic Jews long for faithful relationships. Loyalty is a fruit of friendship. Church leaders should demonstrate their loyalty to the Messianic Jews, especially when the movement is under attack from both Christian and Jewish opponents.

We must not betray our Messianic brothers and sisters again for the sake of any other relationship as happened in the first century.

- **Acceptance of the potential** – We need to communicate our support for the movement and how much potential we see in them – even though the movement is still in an early stage of development. With our prophetic eyes, we should see the potential of the 'Church of the Jews' of tomorrow in them.

- **Acknowledgment of the 'Older Brothers'** – This acceptance includes another element – to see in them the 'Older Brother'. 'To the Jew first,' says the Apostle Paul. This also speaks about their position in the Body of Messiah. Even though the Messianic Jews are coming in as the latest in Church history – their apostolic Messianic ancestors were the first to whom the risen Messiah revealed Himself. What a great mystery! Although for centuries they had ceased to exist, the authority of the first generation of the Jewish apostles somehow still rests on them. Because of this, they rightly deserve the 'first place' as the 'Older Brothers.' This role as the 'Older Brother' is not foremost a structural position but entitles them, with honour, to bring their part as a healing ministry into the whole

Body. This will have consequences for how the Church will operate in the last days.

- **Respect for their autonomy** – Gentile Christianity must recognise and support the autonomous existence of the Messianic Movement. No oversight or control over Messianic congregations by a Gentile Church is acceptable. Messianic congregations may be protected under a Gentile umbrella – but they should never be under the complete authority of any Christian denomination. To become the Jewish part of the Church – the Gentiles, in all their care, need to give them the 'room' to exercise their God-given priestly role within the Body of Christ. *Only out of this autonomy will they be able to relate in the right way to the different parts of Christianity, and to minister in the right form to their own Jewish people.*

- **Freedom and space** – The Christian churches need to give a great deal of space to the Messianic Movement so that it can freely develop its theological identity and its structural forms. Even though we, as Gentiles, sometimes think we know what would be best for them in their development, it is dramatically counterproductive to dominate them with our good intentions. We should offer our theological heritage and our ecclesial and pastoral experiences – but they, themselves, need to receive from the Holy Spirit how to relate all of this to their particular calling.

- **Transmission of 'spiritual treasure'** – As Christian churches, we have a lot to offer. There is a collective treasure in the many Gentile Christian traditions which have been preserved, some of which even reflect the Church's Judeo-Christian-heritage which has waited for the Messianic Jews to unpack those Jewish treasures. Our offer must be a free offer – without any pressure on our part.

- **Support** – The Messianic Movement needs all the support it can get from the historic and independent churches. The more support they receive – the healthier they will be. This also involves financial support and it seems right and just that, as the Church throughout history often prospered from what was taken away from the Jews by force, now the churches should be generous in 'giving back'.

- **Intercession for the leadership** – Support must be carried out at all levels, particularly through the ministry of intercession. The leadership of the Messianic Movement is under continuous stress. This is especially true for the leadership in Israel who are surrounded by Jewish groups opposed to the movement. Because many of the Messianic leaders are confronted with so many tensions from inside and outside the movement, many of them give up. This pressure can also cause their families to collapse and their congregations to lose their shepherds.

- **Discernment of Spirits** – This may almost sound as if I am contradicting what I said before about 'autonomy' and 'freedom.' Nevertheless, to support the health of the movement fully, we Gentiles need to discern if a group is authentic and is able to be a partner to us. Pseudo-messianic-sects are more of a problem than a blessing. This kind of hard discernment can be a great support, although it may initially appear as inappropriate judgement from the outside. Unfortunately, too many false sects exist, creating criticism against the legitimate. Such sectarian groups often consist of very few Jewish members and masses of Israel focused Gentiles who try to pretend some Jewish ancestry. Such groups are operating from a shallow theological foundation, focusing on Jewish folklore and sometimes even on legalistic Torah observation. They cause a lot of confusion within Christianity and disqualify the real Messianic Movement through their misleading witness.

- **Advocacy within the Gentile world** – The Biblical truths of the end-time return of the Messianic Community need to be promulgated within the Gentile world. There is a need for theologians and Church leaders to become advocates for the movement, particularly within the Arab Christian Communities.

The work of the Holy Spirit – The phenomenon of the Messianic movement should not be seen in isolation. There have been four surprises of the Holy Spirit in the last century: without any precedence in Christian history the Holy Spirit was poured out over the faithful.

1. It began with the Pentecostal revival in the early days of the 1900s,

2. followed by the Neo-Pentecostal outpouring over parts of the historic churches with Reformation

background. Around 550 million Christians were involved in this largest revival of all Christian history.

3. In 1967 the Pentecostal movement finally reached the Catholic Church. What followed was the most dramatic Church renewal. Around 120 million Catholics have been touched by it in the last 50 years. The Charismatic movement brought new elements into the life of those who joined: a new dimension of prayer and intimacy with God through the baptism in the Holy Spirit; a rediscovering of the 'supernatural' charisms of the apostolic age and a greater openness for signs and wonders within the daily realities of life; a deeper understanding of the Scriptures; a passion for evangelism; a hunger for discipleship and for living in radical 'committed communities', an ecumenical desire and, last but not least, a new eschatological hope.

4. It is not an accident that the Messianic movement also saw the beginning of its sudden, extraordinary, surge of growth at the end of the 60s.

These four surprises of the Spirit are inter-related. A large part of the Messianic movement shares in this Charismatic experience and spirituality. All the Charismatic experiences impacted the growth of the movement significantly. Particularly, the very concrete eschatological hope of Messianic Jews for a fulfilment of all the Old-Testament prophecies is an integral part of Charismatic experience. Charismatic spirituality allows for an expectation of the impossible, even the hope for a full maturing of the movement and a final unity between the Jewish and the Gentile part of the Church according to the One-New-Man vision of Ephesians 2.

In May of 2017 Pope Francis invited 50,000 delegates of the Catholic Charismatic Renewal movement from all regions of the earth to celebrate the 'Golden Jubilee' in Rome. Again, it was not by accident that the Pope insisted on having the main gathering celebrated as an ecumenical event at the place of the Christian martyrs of the first three centuries, the Circo Massimo. And it was also not an accident that the Pope insisted on having two representatives of the Messianic movement sitting next to him on the platform. He wanted to demonstrate to this celebrating audience how much he considers the Messianic movement to be a significant factor in the coming renewal of the Church and its preparation for the end times.

EIGHT

THE INITIATIVE 'TOWARDS A SECOND COUNCIL OF JERUSALEM (TJCII)

IT WAS A HOT SUMMER DAY in 1995 when young Rabbi Marty Waldman, Secretary General of the 'Union of Messianic Jewish Congregations' (UMJC) was sitting in his office in Dallas, Texas, to prepare a teaching on Acts 15, about the Council in Jerusalem. There he had a 'vision'. Rabbi Marty saw a need for another Council in Jerusalem. This Second Council should reverse what had been accomplished at the First. This time the Gentiles would have to welcome back the Jews as their Older Brothers.

Rabbi Waldman, pastor of one of the largest Messianic congregations in the USA, contacted his closer Messianic and Christian friends to hear their opinion. All of them were in favour. This is from God,' they said. A group of pioneers began preparations for such an event to be accomplished within the next 10 years. The title of the project was to be: 'Jerusalem Council II'. This hope for a quick fulfilment changed into ecclesial realism when a year later a Catholic priest and theologian, Msgr. Dr. Peter Hocken, and an Anglican Canon, Dr. Brian Cox, joined the group. Their knowledge about the lengthy timescale of preparations for such convocations of all of Christianity, including the historic Churches, suggested the need of an addition to the title of the initiative. The name of the initiative was thus changed into: '**Towards** Jerusalem Council II'.

In 1997 the group started a tour throughout Europe to meet with Church leaders and also visit places of significant Jewish suffering. A key encounter during the tour happened when the group met **Cardinal Christoph Schönborn**, the Archbishop of Vienna. Deeply touched personally by the witness of the Messianic leaders, the Cardinal opened the door for more meetings with high representatives of the Catholic Church. Further pilgrimages led the group to Spain, Rome, Istanbul/Constantinople, Nicea, Auschwitz and Israel.

In the year 2000 the initiative adopted its current structure. TJCII is led by an International Council of Leaders (ILC), 24 men, 12 of them representing the different parts of the Messianic movement, 12 of them representing many different Churches and streams within Christianity. By intention, right from the beginning, TJCII wanted to be a prophetic sign of a solid but also a broad unity between the different Messianic parties and the many Christian denominations. TJCII always wanted to integrate representatives of all the main Churches even at the risk of putting off some of the more insular, independent Churches or Messianic congregations who cannot contribute to this large vision of unity in the Body of the Messiah. The members of the ILC are committed, through a covenant relationship, to devoting their lives to this task and to journeying together. They meet at least once a year in Jerusalem. Four members of the ILC, the **International Executive**, are co-ordinating the work of the initiative throughout the year to help to implement the decisions taken by the ILC.

The Vision of TJCII – The One New Man - In the centre of the initiative is the vision of Ephesians 2 about the unity of Jews and Gentiles in the one Body of the Messiah. It is true that the atonement of the cross had removed the barrier in principle; had bridged over the rift between the two. Jesus' sacrificial death had pulled down the wall of division between the people of the covenant and the nations longing for God´s Kingdom to come. Nevertheless, the work of the Messiah has to be completed by the realisation of this relationship on all levels and dimensions of communitarian life. Reconciliation has to be realised in the one Body of the Messiah and in all possible scenarios where Jews and Gentiles share their faith and life together. This One New Man vision is the down payment and foundation for restoration of the peace and unity of mankind. As has been already expressed: as long as these two parts of the Body of the Messiah are kept apart, all striving for reconciliation between denominations and people groups will only remain as pieces in the puzzle. The healing of the first split is the key for Church and world reconciliation. Many other and important issues are indirectly connected to the work of TJCII: how we relate to the debate about Eretz Israel; how we see Zionism; how peace will come in the Middle East and other related topics. But we want to concentrate on this One New Man issue. Because of the dominance of this topic, we often speak of it as the 'single focus' of TJCII.

A Moving Tabernacle. Whenever TJCII starts its work in a new region of the world the ILC meets there together. The experience is very often the same. At those gatherings, the Christian leaders from most of the denominations present in the region experience something of this 'unity' according to the One New Man mystery described in Ephesians 2. In a prophetic way the ILC already represents the future unity of Jew and Gentile. It seems that the Spirit indwelling this prophetic sign is able to calm down even long-term conflicts between Christian churches, at least for the moment, as a sign of hope.

The Elders of Jerusalem. The ILC works closely together with a group of Messianic Jewish Elders in Jerusalem and from the whole land of Israel. These leaders have to be the welcoming partners for the ILC to build their work on solid relationships and developed trust with the Messianic leaders in the Land. At the present four Messianic pastors, Benjamin Berger, Marcel Rebiai, Daniel Juster and Avi Mizrachi coordinate this collaboration between the ILC and its counterpart in Israel. Some of the administration of TJCII has already moved to an office in Jerusalem in the Clal-building with its prayer tower, which is partly administrated by some Messianic Jewish congregations.

As important as the relationships with the Jewish partners in Israel are, they can be equally difficult when some of the Messianic Israelis share quite deep mistrust, especially towards the participation of Catholic or Orthodox representatives within the ILC. There is often a fear of being dominated by those large Church bodies and their previous 'questionable teaching'.

The International TJCII Office in Dallas. The Messianic-

Jewish Synagogue 'Baruch Ha Shem' in Dallas, Texas, played a significant role in developing this initiative right from the start. Today Rabbi Marty Waldman continues to serve as the Secretary General of TJCII and his staff looks after the international business. This includes a Board of Directors for the finances. As the work develops in other continents a continental office always needs to be established and equipped with the necessary staff.

Intercession. As TJCII is first and foremost a spiritual initiative, intercession is central to all its activities. This kind of reconciliation has to overcome enormous demonic barriers. We have already spoken about it. In all TJCII regions, the forming of a group of committed intercessors is the first action we take. For this role we recruit mature believers from both sides with a lot of experience in the area of intercession and spiritual warfare rather than highly emotionally motivated 'Israel-fans'. The main purpose of these intercessory groups is to deal in prayer with the spiritual strongholds connected to Jewish history in the particular nations or regions where TJCII operates.

Theology. In each region we try to form a group of theologians who are able to 'translate' the overall vision for the unity of Jew and Gentile in one Church, into the theological 'language' of the particular culture and/or theology of the respective Christian denominations. The more we are able to explain our theological focus with solid arguments, in academic terms, the better equipped we are to go into difficult confrontations with Church leaders and theologians. To produce this kind of theological literature is one of the main tasks for the 'Theological Working Groups'.

Diplomatic work. The theological understanding has to be brought to the knowledge of those who are making the decisions both in the Church and in society. The final goal is to convince them and persuade them to collaborate with us. This means working on relationships with these opinion leaders, getting their interest and respect and winning them for our cause.

Promotion. While the diplomatic work often has to be accomplished in a clandestine atmosphere, it needs some publicity to expand the work of TJCII. A rather broad group of people must be reached with the message. Conferences, consultations, public penitential discussions, booklets and brochures, information evenings on academic ground or in congregations, media-work – all of this helps to promote the One New Man cause. So often we are confronted with the rather emotional comment: why haven't we heard about this foundational truth earlier? One task is to win the Messianic circles in Israel, which is difficult enough. Even more difficult is it to convince Arab-Christian circles.

Working on all continents. According to historic, cultural and language differences we have to establish the work of TJCII on all the continents and sub-continents.

In **Europe** we have established an office in Vienna, right at the geographic heart of Europe, with the special bridge building role of Austria between the East and the West, within a nation with a particularly difficult history with the Jewish people. We have now established 'National TJCII teams' and intercessory groups in about 13 European countries, which work inter-relatedly, but are at the same time self-governing because of the great language challenges we have to face in Europe. There is great collaboration between them and the European director and the office in Vienna.

TJCII North-America is co-ordinated from the International Office in Dallas, Texas. There are several regional TJCII centres around the nation and in Canada.

The work in South-America has to respect the language barrier between the Spanish speaking nations and Brazil. Brazil is the country where TJCII is most established. The Messianic partners of TJCII are all connected with each other through the largest Messianic congregation in the city of Belo Horizonte, which is specially focused on the work with Marrano descendants. The TJCII leadership in Brazil consists of well- known Christian 'bridge-builders', among them members of the Protestant 'Sisterhood of Mary', who understood the vision and saw how much this One New Man policy could help heal the religious divisions between Catholics and Evangelicals on the subcontinent.

The work in Asia. For a few decades now there has been a growing interest among the many different Christian streams in Asia in the role of Israel and for the reconciliation work of TJCII in particular. Whole mega-churches, large congregations, house-church movements and influential Christian universities in South Korea are eager to collaborate with TJCII. There is a growing connection with the Chinese Church and its 'Back to Jerusalem' vision.

The work in **Africa** goes out from a particular intercession initiative in Nairobi, Kenya, called the 'Vanguard'. Because the female leader of this group, Elisabeth Kamau, is an Anglican deacon many of our TJCII contacts there are with Anglican leaders in the neighbouring countries. Among the African Christians in general there exists a particularly strong identification with the Jewish people and the relationship between them.

The future of TJCII rests to a high degree on a movement of young leaders called the **'Now Generation'**. What started as an initiative of young men and women in Europe, identifying with the One New Man vision, collects more and more young people in their 30s and 40s to support the work of the 'Fathers and Mothers' of TJCII at all levels. Many of them are already serving as Missionaries of TJCII to their generation.

NINE

THE VISION OF A SECOND COUNCIL OF JERUSALEM

THERE IS HOPE FOR A SOLEMN CONVOCATION, for an official event in some way similar to the *First Jerusalem Council* described in Acts 15. This in a sense is the ultimate goal for the TJCII initiative. A working title could be the *Second Council of Jerusalem*. It should be a formal assembly of all parts of the Body of Christ. It needs to be an assembly where there is enough representation of each denominational leadership so that the entire Body is able to come to consensus and speak with one voice. This gathering may be without precedent in Church history and it will be unique in its form, not a copy of any other Church's council in history, and not comparable to any other international leadership conference. At such a universal convocation of Christian leaders, the recognition of the 'Church of the Jews' by the Gentile Churches must finally take place.

- **It is the inverse of the *First Council (Acts 15)*** – At the *First Council of Jerusalem*, the Apostles made the decision that the Jewish believers had to make room for the Gentile believers without requiring that they become Jews. Such a *Second Council* would have to be the inverse of that. The Gentile Christian leaders would have formally to recognise the resurrection of the Messianic Body and to enter into full communion with the 'Church of the Circumcision.' Such an event will only happen under a special leading of the Holy

Spirit. Only the Holy Spirit can show the churches how such a communion, recognised by all denominations, could take place.

- **Great Humility is required** – Such a *Council* will only take place when humility, brokenness and repentance open up the hearts of men and women and bring forth the ability to welcome the Messianic Movement as a gift of God. For this openness to happen, all Gentile Christian leaders have to offer back to the Lamb their 'crowns,' which might also include their positions and titles - to use the image of Rev 4: 10. For moving into a deeper level of unity it is unhelpful to insist on the status of being an 'archbishop,' or 'superintendent,' or even an 'apostle'. Holding on to titles will not help when this re-ordering of relationships within the whole Body takes place.

God will challenge all leaders, whoever they may be: *'Come down from your thrones, give up your positions, be ready to lose your reputations and kneel before my sheep – offering your servant-attitude.'* This is what the Holy Spirit will require from all of us. Otherwise, the Gentile Church will never comprehend that the Messianic Jews are a part of the unified Body. Only when we are humble and broken, are we able to make room for the Jews in the Church. This overwhelming humility will be the fruit of a great deal of prayer.

- **The Elder Brothers need to be accepted** – Receiving Messianic Jews just as an interesting religious phenomenon is not enough! They will have to be received as the 'Elder Brothers'. They must not form just a new denomination among the thousands that already exist. Being our 'Elder Brothers' means a special place, a position most of all of spiritual authority, representing somehow the spiritual authority of the first Jewish believers. On them rests a particular authority, coming in a mysterious way directly from the lineage of the Apostles, Peter, Paul, James and others.

- **The Messianic Jews have a particular role within the Body** – Receiving them as 'Elder Brothers', corresponds to the re-establishment of the Jewish part of the Church. Such a *Second Council of Jerusalem* will result in a dramatic 're-ordering' of the whole Body. There will be a deep unity – going deeper and further than any classic ecumenism so far. *This new depth of unity will take place because the Messianic witness will challenge all Gentile Churches in their relationships with one another*. The first split wounded Church unity profoundly. All later 'breakaways' within Gentile Christianity were at least indirectly related to this original split. As the first split became a matter of course, setting free a 'division-virus', conversely, this reunion of Jew and Gentile will be a blessing for the Church and to the world, bringing unity and peace.

- **It will bring healing from the wounds of separation** – The attitude of humility and repentance will allow the Messianic Jews to take their place within the Body. It will bring forth a level of healing for the broken Body of the Messiah like never before. Wounds of separation between Christian denominations, some of them burdening the relationships for centuries, will be removed. A climate of embrace and forgiveness will allow new beginnings. There will be supernatural healing power to restore the trust between fathers and sons and sons and fathers (Mal. 3: 24).

- **An ecumenical earthquake** – Such a *Second Council* will be an ecumenical earthquake! But this reconciliation does not occur miraculously all at once! It will be the fruit of decades of preparation and a thorough reconciliation work between Jews and Gentiles, and within the Gentile denominations as well. This *Second Council* will be the completion of many decades of hard 'ecumenical labour' and should bring a lasting harvest of all the many previous existing Christian convocations and unity-conferences. During this process the Holy Spirit will have to reveal new ways for the Church to realise unity. There exists a Biblical example of the principle *'unity in diversity.'* The twelve tribes of Israel were, despite all their differences, able to be one chosen people of God. Their differences added riches to their unity rather than lessening the level of it. Could this be a model for the 'One Church' - united in essentials and, at the same time, colourful in diverse forms of ecclesial and liturgical expressions?

- **Unity in diversity & unity through diversity** – There is a special anointing over the Jewish people. As the Jewish part of the Church joins, they could become a model for how this principle of 'unity in diversity' works. The Jewish concept of unity is never uniformity. What will bring us together in the same Body will be the intense love and passion for the Messiah and all that we believe about him. At the same time, being different will become a blessing and will not be a threat. Diversity reveals the creativity of the Holy Spirit. God´s Spirit rejoices in all the variations, reminding the Church that her different expressions reveal something of the fullness of the revelation of Christ (John 16:13-15). *Unity in diversity & unity through diversity* in the Church will finally even become an inspiration for pathways to peace and unity in the secular society.

- **Jerusalem will be the centre** – A *Second Jerusalem Council* will move the 'centre of the Body of Christ' from Rome, Constantinople, Geneva, London or Springfield to Jerusalem, the City of the Great King! As a result of such a *Council*, the prophecy of Isaiah 2:2-5 could become reality. Maybe it would not be realised in its ultimate eschatological form (which would involve the return of the Eternal King to the throne of David) but it could be a strong sign to the nations when all churches decide to organise their unity out of Jerusalem instead of other places. To have the Council in Jerusalem would require first and foremost that, in Jerusalem, there would be an established and united Messianic Jewish and Gentile eldership, who would welcome the delegations from the denominations for such an event. This role of Jerusalem elders as hosts would be even more important when the Gentile Church leaders bring their headquarters to this Jewish capital. Before reaching such a goal - much intercession and healing is necessary. All efforts made in our days in the city of David to bring forth unity among the Messianic Jewish eldership and between them and the Gentile elders and bishops are worth the price. These are the necessary preparations for us to realise the ultimate role of Jerusalem one day. Already now all Christian denominations should re-orient themselves to see Jerusalem as the focus of salvation history.

- **There will be a re-examination of many parts of our respective theologies in the light of this development** – Such a *Council* will also be a time of a significant re-examination of Christian teaching. Not that the teaching of the churches was wrong! The Holy Spirit protected the Church through all these centuries, without its Jewish component, so it did not fall into heresy. *But, to use a picture - all of our Church beliefs will be thrown into the 'washing machine' of the Holy Spirit to be purified.* The presence of the Messianic Jews, and their Hebrew mind-set, will change some of our perspectives. Our unity as Gentiles will make a big difference in the way we teach about Biblical truth. Everything will be purified. In the presence of the Messianic Jews, all systematic theology, all liturgies, all of church practice will be re-evaluated. This new attitude towards teaching will not start at the *Council*. A lot of that will be done before such a *Council*, as a preparation, as Christianity recognises more and more the Jewish roots of her faith. To be clear: it is not about 'Judaising' but rather about seeing our Church teaching within an enlarged framework of belief in respect for the Jewish roots of Christian faith. It needs a certain quality of relationship among Christian leaders and theologians to bring the many and rich Christian traditions together into full harmony.

- **To prepare for the Second Coming** – *'No one knows the hour, not even the Son, only the Father.'* (Mat. 24:36). Without putting the final events and the final hour of ultimate salvation into human hands such a *Council* would have an eschatological dimension to it even though it will still happen in the sphere of human responsibility. In fact, such a Council may be the most important step to prepare this 'now-united Church' to become the Bride with fewer spots and wrinkles; prepared for the end-time evangelistic harvest; prepared for all the persecution under which the Body will be cleansed; prepared to reveal her bridal beauty; prepared to stand against the attacks of the enemy which will prove to be more severe and destructive than at any time before. Only when the Church is united will it be able to completely direct all her energies towards this required holiness and sanctification which alone enables the Body to fulfil its eschatological destiny.

- **The realisation of the 'One New Man'** – What has been accomplished by the blood of the Messiah to establish this 'One New Man' according to Ephesians 2, should be finally and formally reached in such a *Council*. This will bring the Church more than ever before into its 'fullness'. This development will be the greatest witness to mankind. It may lead to mass conversions among the nations and among those in Israel who had until then opposed the recognition of Jesus as their Messiah. It will be a witness for reconciliation and peace for all of mankind and will promote dramatic political changes in the direction of human rights and dignity. It will be an overwhelming witness for the redemptive power of the blood of the Messiah to all religions.

- **The last miracle of Jesus before his Second Coming** – In the autumn of 2006, a TJCII delegation consisting of Messianic Jewish, Protestant and Catholic theologians met for the first time for a theological encounter with Romanian Orthodox Church leaders in an old monastery in the snowy mountains of Central Romania. To our astonishment, four Bishops, 40 priests and at least ten lay theologians came together with a great number of interested lay leaders from Eastern Orthodox renewal movements. In spite of beginning well, the encounter quickly turned into a conflict. As TJCII representatives we felt a lot of prejudice, almost hostility. The breakthrough happened on the last day of the conference. A Romanian Orthodox Bishop came forward to the pulpit to give his statement.

The Bishop, himself a well-known New Testament scholar, was speaking about the resurrection of Lazarus from the Gospel of John. The resurrection of Lazarus, he emphasised, was the last miracle Jesus performed before His own resurrection. The fact that the Messianic Movement has come *'to life again from the dead'* may be the last miracle Jesus performs before His Second Coming. The Lord resurrected them from the dead. But we, as Gentile Christians, need to lead them out of their grave. We have to pull aside the big stones before the grave, which are blocking their way out. We have to unbind them from everything that hinders them from receiving the full freedom the Messiah intended for them. And the bishop finished with an almost prophetic statement: *'When the Jews finally come out of their grave, what else will this be, other than a global celebration of restoration, of coming home, home to Zion. Maybe this could be the Second Council of Jerusalem?'*

Suggested Reading

Bagatti, Belarmino; *The Church from the Circumcision*; 2; Rome 1984

Ben-Chorin, Schalom; *Messianische Juden. Judenchristen in Israel.* In: Ders.: Theologia Judaica. Gesammelte Aufsätze; 2. Bd; Verena Lenzen (Hg); Tübingen 1992

Ben-Chorin, Schalom; *Die Erwählung Israels.* Ein theologisch-politischer Traktat; München 1993

Bennett, Ramon; *When Day and Night Cease*; Jerusalem 1992

Berger, Benjamin u. Berger, Ruben; *Der Weg. Der gute Weg unseres Lebens mit Jeschua im Land Israel*; Toffen 2010

Berger, Benjamin; *Die Wiederherstellung. Der König kommt und baut sein Reich*; Toffen 2012

Berger, Benjamin; *Jeschua von Nazareth. König der Juden*; Toffen 2016

Berger, David u. Wyschogrod, Michael; J*ews and 'Jewish Christianity'*; New York 1978

Binder, Heribert; *'Geburtsurkunde' der messianisch-jüdischen Bewegung?* Geheimnisvolle Dokumente im Unitäts-Archiv Herrnhut; in: Fichtenbauer, Johannes (Hg.); Festschrift für Peter Hocken zum 80. Geburtstag; noch unveröffentlicht.

Bronstein, David; *Judaism and Christianity. Are They the Same*; Florida 1963

Brown, Michael L.; *Answering Jewish Objections to Jesus*; Grand Rapids 2000

Cohn-Sherbok, Dan; *Messianic Judaism*; London-New York 2000.

Corey, Muriel; *From Rabbi to Bishop. The Biography of the Right Reverend Michael Salomon Alexander*; London 1956

Dalman, Gustaf u. Schulze, Adolf; *Zinzendorf und Lieberkühn. Studien zur Geschichte der Judenmission*; Leipzig 1903

Danielou, Jean; *The Theology of Jewish Christianity*; London 1964

Finto, Don; *Your People Shall Be My People*; Ventura 2001

Fischer, John; *Sharing Israel's Messiah*; Chicago 1978

Friedman, Elias; *Jewish Identity*; New York 1987

Frydland, Rachmiel; *What the Rabbis Know About the Messiah*; Columbus 1991

Gartenhaus, Jacob; *Famous Hebrew Christians*; Grand Rapids 1979.

Gerloff, Johannes; *Messianische Juden in Israel. Mythen und Fakten*; In: Bibel und Gemeinde; 4/1999

Gruber, Daniel; *The Church and the Jews*; Springfield 1991

Hafner, Georg u. Schapira, Ester; *Israel ist an allem schuld. Warum der Judenstaat so gehasst wird*; Köln 2015

Harvey, Richard; *Mapping Messianic Jewish Theology. A constructive Approach*; Colorado Springs 2009

SUGGESTED READING

Henrix, Hans Hermann; *Gottes Ja zu Israel; Studien zu Kirche und Israel*; Bd. 23; Berlin-Aachen 2005

Henrix, Hans Hermann u. Rendtorff, Rolf (Hg); *Die Kirchen und das Judentum. Dokumente von 1945-1985*; 2; Paderborn-München 1989

Hocken, Peter; *The Strategy of the Spirit*; 2; Guilford-Surrey 1998.

Hocken, Peter; *The Unity of the Spirit*; Cambridge 2001

Hocken, Peter; *The Challenges of the Pentecostal, Charismatic and Messianic Jewish Movements*; Burlington 2009

Hocken, Peter; Pentecost and Parousia: Charismatic Renewal, Christian Unity, and the Coming Glory; Eugene 2014

Hocken, Peter; *Azusa, Rome and Zion. Pentecostal Faith, Catholic Reform, and Jewish Roots*; Eugene 2016

Hocken, Peter u. Justin, Daniel; *The Messianic Jewish Movement. An Introduction*; Dallas 2013

Hocken, Peter; *The Marranos*; Dallas 2013

Hocken, Peter u. Justin, Daniel; *Towards Jerusalem Council II. Vision, Origin and Documents*; Dallas 2013

Intrater, Keith (Asher) u. Juster, Daniel; *Israel, The Church and the Last Days*; Shippensburg 1990.

Intrater, Keith (Asher); *From Iraq to Armageddon*; Shippensburg 1991

Juster, Daniel; *Growing to Maturity*; Shippensburg 1982

Juster, Daniel; Revelation. *The Passover Key*; Shippensburg 1991

Juster, Daniel; *Jewish Roots. A Foundation of Biblical Theology*; 2 rev.; Shippensburg 1995

Hagner, Donald; *The Jewish Reclamation of Jesus. Analysis and critic of modern Jewish study of Jesus*; Grand Rapids 1984

Heschel, Abraham Joshua; I*srael – Echo der Ewigkeit*; Neukirchen-Vluyn 1988

Hornung, Andreas; *Messianische Juden zwischen Kirche und Volk Israel. Entwicklung und Begründung ihres Selbstverständnisses*; Gießen-Basel 1995

Huisjen, Albert; *The Homefront of Jewish Missions*; Grand Rapids 1962

Kaufmann, Thomas; *Luthers Juden*; Stuttgart 2014

Soulen, Kendal; *The God of Israel and Christian Theology*; Minneapolis 1996

Kinzer, Mark S.; *The Nature of Messianic Judaism. Judaism as Genus, Messianic as Species*; Grand Rapids 2000

Kinzer, Mark S.; *Postmissionary Messianic Judaism. Redefining Christian Engagement with the Jewish People*; Grand Rapids 2005

Kinzer, Mark S.; *Israel's Messiah and the People of God. A Vision for Messianic Jewish Covenant Fidelity*; Grand Rapids 2011

Kinzer, Mark S.; *Searching Her Own Mystery. Nostra Aetate, the Jewish People, and the Identity of the Church*; Eugene 2015

Kinzer, Mark S.; *Jerusalem Crucified, Jerusalem Risen. The Resurrected Messiah, the Jewish People, and the Land of Promise*; Eugene 2018

Kirchenamt der EKD (Hg.); *Christen und Juden I-III. Die Studien der Evangelischen Kirche in Deutschland 1975-2000*; Gütersloh 2002

Kjaer-Hansen, Kai u. Kvarme, Ole Christian; *Messianische Juden. Judenchristen in Israel*; Erlangen 1983

Kjaer-Hansen, Kai u. Skjott, Bodil F.; *Facts & Myths about the Messianic Congregations in Israel*; Jerusalem 1999

Kjaer-Hansen, Kai; *Joseph Rabinowitz and the Messianic Movement*; Grand Rapids 1995

Laepple, Ulrich (Hg); *Messianische Juden. Eine Provokation*. Mit Beiträgen von Richard Harvey, Peter Hirschberg, Ulrich Laepple, Hanna Rucks, Swen Schönheit, Hans-Joarchim und Rita Scholz; Göttingen 2016

Liberman, Paul; *The Fig Tree Blossoms*; Indianola 1976

Lindsay, Mark; *Barth, Israel and Jesus. Karl Barth´s Theology of Israel*; Aldershot 2007

Lohfink, Norbert; *Der niemals gekündigte Bund. Exegetische Gedanken zum christlich-jüdischen Gespräch*; Freiburg 1989

May, Fritz; *Aufbruch im Heiligen Land. Messianische Juden in Israel. Wer sie sind – was sie wollen – wie sie diskriminiert werden*; 2; Asslar 1998

Marquardt, Friedrich-Wilhelm; *'Feinde um unseretwillen'. Das jüdische Nein und die christliche Theologie*; in: Von der Osten-Sacken, Peter (Hg); Treue zur Thora. Beiträge zur Mitte des christlich-jüdischen Gesprächs. Festschrift für Günther Harder; Berlin 1986, 174-193

Meyer, Louis; *Famous Hebrew Christians of the Nineteenth Century*; 2; New York-Toronto 1983

Moltmann, Jürgen; *Der Weg Jesu Christi. Christologie in messianischen Dimensionen*; München 1989

Murray, Iain H.; *The Puritan Hope*; Edinburgh 1971

Pfister, Stefanie; *Messianische Juden in Deutschland. Eine historische und religionssoziologische Untersuchung*; Berlin-Münster 2008

Pritz, Ray A.; *Nazarene Jewish Christianity*. Jerusalem-Leiden 1988

Rausch, David A.; *Messianic Judaism. Its History, Theology, and Polity; Texts and Studies in Religion*; Bd. 14; Lewiston-Queenston 1982

Rausch, David A.; *Zionism Within Early American Fundamentalism 1878-1918*; New York- Toronto 1979

Riggans, Walter; *Yeshua Ben David*; East Sussex 1995

Rucks; Hanna; *Messianische Juden. Geschichte und Theologie der Bewegung in Israel;* Neukirchen 2014

Shishkoff, Eitan; *What about us? The End-Time Calling of Gentiles in Israel's Revival;* Bedford 2013

Schoenfield, Hugh; *The History of Jewish Christianity;* London 1936

Skarsaune, Oskar u. Hvalvik, Reidar (Hg.); *Jewish Believers in Jesus. The Early Centuries;* Peabody 2007

Stern, David H.; *Jewish New Testament Commentary;* Jerusalem-Baltimore 1992

Stern, David H.; *Messianic Jewish Manifesto;* Jerusalem 1987

Stern, David H.; *Restoring the Jewishness of the Gospel;* Jerusalem-Baltimore 1988

Stern, David H.; *Messianic Judaism. A Modern Movement with An Ancient Past;* Clarksville 2007

Tapie, Matthew; *Aquinas on Israel and the Church. The Question of Supersessionism in the Theology of Thomas Aquinas;* Cambridge 2015

Tatai, Istvan; *The Church and Israel. In Search of a new model in post-holocaust theology;* Budapest 2010

Thomas, Evan; *The Messianic Community of Israel. An Overview;* unpublished paper; 2002

Tomson, Peter J.; *Paul and the Jewish Law*; Maastricht-Minneapolis 1990

Tück, Jan Heiner; *Das Konzil und die Juden. 50 Jahre 'Nostra Aetate' – Erbe und Auftrag*; in: Communio 4/2015

Van De Poll, Evert W.; *Sacred Times For Chosen People. Development, Analysis and Missiological Significance of Messianic Jewish Holiday Practice*; Zoetermeer 2008

Von der Osten-Sacken, Peter; *Ein Empfehlungsbrief Christi*; in: Questiones Disputatae 238; 2010

Kommission für die religiösen Beziehungen zum Judentum (Hg); *'Denn unwiderruflich sind Gnade und Berufung, die Gott gewährt'. Röm 11,29. Reflexionen zu theologischen Fragestellungen in den katholisch-jüdischen Beziehungen aus Anlass des 50jährigen Jubiläums von 'Nostra aetate' Nr. 4.*; Vatican 2015

Wengst, Klaus; *'Freut euch, ihr Völker, mit Gottes Volk!'. Israel und die Völker als Thema des Paulus. Ein Gang durch den Römerbrief*; Stuttgart 2008

Winer, Robert; *Modern Messianic Jewish History*; 1987

Yaakov, Ariel; *Evangelizing the Chosen People. Mission to the Jews in America. 1880-2000*; London 2000

Zack-Miley, Hanna; *Meine Krone in der Asche. Der Holocaust, die Kraft der Vergebung und der lange Weg zur persönlichen Heilung*; Basel 2014

enc

European Netzwerk der Gemeinschaften /
European Network of Communities
Boltzmanngasse 9, A-1090 Wien
info@e-n-c.org

TJCII-Europe Office
Fritzi Turecek
Boltzmanngasse 9, A-1090 Wien
f.turecek@edw.or.at
www.tjcii.org

About the Author

Johannes Fichtenbauer was born 1956 in Vienna, Austria and holds an MA in Catholic Theology. He serves as head deacon in the Roman Catholic Archdiocese of Vienna under Cardinal Christoph Schönborn and is responsible for the training of permanent deacons. Previously Johannes held a teaching post in a theological institute for the laity.

Johannes has been married to Christi for more than 40 years. They have four adult children, an adopted son, and five grandchildren. Johannes and Christi were involved in the beginnings of the Catholic Charismatic Renewal in Austria in the early 1970's and co-founded an ecumenical charismatic covenant community in Vienna. Johannes is currently president of the 'European Network of Communities' (ENC), a network of over 80 like-minded communities throughout West and East Europe.

Johannes currently serves as chairman on the 'Round Table' for 'Weg der Versöhnung'; (path for reconciliation), which is the broadest ecumenical grass root initiative in Austria. Out of this he also serves on the Steering Committee for 'Together for Europe'.

In addition to his other positions, Johannes is one of the International Elders and the European Director for 'Toward Jerusalem Council II', an initiative for repentance and reconciliation between Christians world-wide and Messianic Jewish believers. Likewise he has taken part in the semi-official dialogue between Messianic Jewish and Catholic Theologians since 2000.

On application to him, the author will be willing to give permission for parts of this book to be reproduced in part or in whole to promote the values of the book and for other teachings. On application, the author will also authorise other language translation rights.
email for authorisation to:
pavol.strezo@gmail.com (Pavol Strežo)

*Further copies of this book
are available from*

*Goodnews Books
Upper Level, St. John's Church
296 Sundon Park Road
Luton, Beds. LU3 3AL UK*

*01582 571011
orders@goodnewsbooks.co.uk
www.goodnewsbooks.co.uk*